■ **Berkeley College**

From the Library

of

WESTCHESTER CAMPUS

99 CHURCH STREET
WHITE PLAINS, NY 10601

THE TWENTIETH CENTURY
HISTORIES OF FASHION

Series edited by
Ieri Attualità

THE TWENTIETH CENTURY
HISTORIES OF FASHION
Tentative titles

WOMAN

 1. Evening dress 1900 ... 1940 (Marco Tosa)
 2. Evening dress 1940 ... (Marco Tosa)
 3. Maternity clothes (Doretta Davanzo Poli)
 4. Skirts & more skirts (Fiora Gandolfi)
 5. Costume jewellery
 6. Shoes for special occasions
 7. Details: sleeves
 8. Strictly personal: corsets and brassières
 9. Petticoats & co.
10. Nightwear
11. Trousers for women
12. Day and evening bags
13. Blouses
14. Large and small hats
15. Hosiery and related items
16. Gloves
17. Cloaks and coats
18. Light coats and raincoats
19. Accessories for ladies: umbrellas and canes
20. Hairstyles
21. You can do anything with fur vol. 1
22. You can do anything with fur vol. 2
23. Casual shoes and boots
24. Afternoon and cocktail dress
25. Shawls, scarfs and silk squares
26. Bridal gowns
27. Work-clothes
28. Beachwear and swimsuits
29. Details: necks and necklines
30. Belts and artificial flowers
31. Suits and daywear
32. Tricot and jersey fashions

CHILDREN

33. Dressed up for a party
34. Girls
35. Children and brats
36. Children's shoes
37. Teenage boys
38. Teenage girls
39. Babies

MEN

40. Men's hats (Giuliano Folledore)
41. Men's furs (Anna Municchi)
42. Trousers & co. (Vittoria de Buzzaccarini)
43. Work-clothes
44. Underwear
45. Shirts
46. Men's accessories: belts, gloves, ties and scarfs
47. Jackets
48. Waistcoats
49. Men's jewellery
50. Raincoats, ponchos and K-ways
51. Umbrellas, sticks and canes
52. Overcoats and coats
53. Pyjamas, robes etc.
54. Knitwear: cardigans and pullovers
55. Sportswear
56. Hairstyles, beards and mustaches
57. Shoes and boots
58. Uniforms
59. Suitcases, briefcases and bags
60. Swimsuits
61. Casualwear: blouson jackets and cabans

SPECIAL ITEMS

62. The handkerchief
63. Buttons
64. Ribbons round the world
65. Leather clothing
66. Jeans
67. T- and polo shirts
68. Glasses

FABRICS

69. Fabrics in fashions: cotton
70. Fabrics in fashions: wool
71. Fabrics in fashions: silk
72. Fabrics in fashions: man-made fabrics

DORETTA DAVANZO POLI

MATERNITY FASHION

ZanfiEditori

ACKNOWLEDGEMENTS

The author would like to thank the following
people for their help:
Enzo and Clara Cassetti
Lia Chinosi
Consorzio Merletti di Burano
Vittoria de Buzzaccarini
Giuseppina Lamberti of Prénatal
Anna Leandro
Domenico Micconi
Stefania Moronato of the Centro Studi di Storia del
Costume e del Tessuto, Palazzo Mocenigo, Venezia
Carla Pandini of LBG Gruppo Creativo
Giuseppe Pellissetti
Giuseppina Reinisch Sullam
Giancarla Rosada of the Assessorato alla
Programmazione Sanitaria del Comune di Venezia
Mattel

PHOTOGRAPHIC CREDITS

Photographs n, 33, 55, 85, 98, 107, 135, 136, 137,
and 167 appear by kind permission of the Centro
Studi di Storia del Tessuto e del Costume, Palazzo
Mocenigo, Venezia.

N. 15, 18 and 45 are from the Picture Archive of the
Fondazione Querini Stampalia, Venezia.

N. 99 and 156 are from the Bertarelli Print Collection,
Milano.

All other illustrations are from the Authoress's private
photograph collection, private collections and the
Ieri Attualità Archive.

Coordination: Vittoria de Buzzaccarini
Iconographic research: Ieri Attualità,
Doretta Davanzo Poli.
Editorial staff: Vittoria de Buzzaccarini,
Elena Vezzalini
Graphic design and cover: Giorgio Trani
Translation: Margaret Kearton - Logos Modena
Original title: Le vesti dell'attesa

ili ZanfiEditori s.r.l.
via Ganaceto 121, 41.100 Modena (Italy)
Tel. 059/222292 - Telex 214614 I

INDEX

To my parents
Carlo Davanzo and Wanda Sgnaolin Bernardi

IN THE BEGINNING

ONCE UPON A TIME

The maternity dress is a modern invention, dating from the time when pregnancy began to be considered as a positive state and a special but natural event which enriched and completed a woman's life, rather than as a "nine months' illness" which could be fatal, or a condition which was by definition shameful because it was the consequence of sexual intercourse.

Until twenty years ago, the Catholic Church required women who had given birth to undertake an act of contrition, receiving them back into the religious life of the community only after they had received purification and benediction.

After all, the Virgin Mary herself, forty days after Christ's birth (Luke 2,21), went to the Temple for the purification with "two doves or small pigeons" for the sacrifice, as required by Jewish law.

In fact, the Bible (Leviticus, 12,1) states: "If a woman becomes pregnant and gives birth to a son, she will be impure for seven days, the one day for each month of her menstrual impurity. On the eighth day the baby will be circumcised, and the mother will remain apart for another thirty-three days to purify her blood: she will not touch any sacred object or go to the sanctuary until her purification is complete." If the child was a girl, the period of spiritual contamination was doubled to two weeks and sixty-six days.

1. Venetian school 14th Century. *Santa Lucia* (detail). Venice, Gallerie dell'Accademia. The line of clothes in the Fourteenth Century was flowing and comfortable. There was no cut at the waistline and dresses were fitted at the breast, then falling into soft folds on the hips.

Given this background, it seems only to be expected that for centuries women felt themselves obliged to spend their pregnancies withdrawn from society, terrified by the fear of death which often struck during childbirth, making their wills, and taking no interest in their clothing or their physical appearance.

And for this reason there were no special

2. Venetian school 14th Century. *Figura allegorica.* Venice, Gallerie dell'Accademia.
Here again, the taste for references to motherhood in this period is very clear. The dress, in yellow satin with gold decoration, featuring low neckline reaching from shoulder to shoulder and tight-fitting sleeves, rests on the breasts and belly, showing their form.

3. Venetian school, 14th Century. *Madonna del Parto.* Venice, Gallerie dell'Accademia.
The Virgin, visibly pregnant, wears a pink tunic with no cut at the waistline which flares from the bust downwards. The full pale blue mantle, decorated with oriental motifs, is unable to conceal her pregnant belly.

8

2.

clothes for pregnant women as such until the second quarter of the Twentieth Century.

IN THE FAMILY WAY

If we trace the history of women's clothing over the ages, we will notice an alternation of styles which adapt themselves or allude in some way to pregnancy, with others which are absolutely incompatible with this temporary physical state.

Styles of the first type feature loose-fitting garments with a high waistline which soften the shape of the pregnant woman's body, making it attractive. These contrast with the opposing trends, which call for tight-fitting garments and skimpy bodices which look clumsy and inelegant when they are gradually enlarged. There are certainly grounds for maintaining that the first type of dress coincided with periods of history when women were treated with respect: from the Middle Ages to the beginning of the Sixteenth Century they were idealized as delicate, virtuous angels, virgins and mothers; in the mid-Seventeenth

Century their intellectual qualities were discovered; after the French revolution this subject came to the surface again, and the end of the Nineteenth Century saw the beginning of the struggles for emancipation.

Clothing of the second type predominated in periods when women were viewed only as the object of men's erotic and sensual passions.

THE PREGNANT MADONNA

During the Fourteenth Century, straight cut tunics with varying degrees of ornamentation, long, tight sleeves, sweeping skirts and a waistline reaching up towards the breasts, gave all women a maternal appearance.

4. GIOTTO (1266-1337) *Corteo nuziale della Vergine*, Padua, Cappella degli Scrovegni.
The Virgin wears a loose-fitting sleeveless surcoat over a dress in a similar colour which is glimpsed at the lower front hem and in the train. Her pregnancy, in its early stages, is emphasized by the position of her body (with the stomach thrust slightly forward) and the folds of the surcoat, which are held raised in front of her.

10

A sort of round-necked sleeveless surcoat or robe, partially open down the sides, which could be worn over the basic gown, made things even more confusing. The Giotto Madonna in the Scrovegni Chapel in Padua is represented as clearly pregnant not only in the *Visitazione* and the *Sposalizio* but also in the *Annunciazione*.

The tight-fitting line of the waist-length bodice worn during the first half of the Fifteenth Century was adapted to pregnancy by slackening the laces on the front and undoing the side seams: this is realistically portrayed in the *Madonna del Parto* at Monterchi by Piero della Francesca.

Pisanello, Crivelli and Bellini are just a few of the many painters who have left us specific, detailed information on costume. Thanks to them, we are able to state that in the middle of the Fifteenth Century waistlines once again moved upwards. So the waists of the regal "hoppelandes" in latticed velvet, lined with ermine, or the overgarments opening at an acute angle over full petticoats, were all decidedly high.

High waists can be found all over Europe, emphasized by the fashion for skirts in a contrasting colour, which led the overgarment to be lifted, almost bunched up, and draped over the stomach. This graceful, very feminine form can be confused with that of the pregnant woman, to whom it also comes naturally to rest a proud, protective hand on her swollen belly.

The most famous picture showing clothing of this type is Van Eyck's The Marriage of Giovanni Arnolfini and Giovanna Cenami. The amount of bulky fabric concentrated on the woman's belly gives the impression that she is pregnant, but the fact that countless other pictures of the period show women clothed in the same way and in the same posture has led to doubts being raised. Black and Garland comment as follows in their history of costume: "It used to be thought that the woman was pregnant, but this effect derives from the fact that the skirt is raised at the front, since the amount of fabric used in

11

5. GIOTTO (1266-1337) *Matrimonio della Vergine*. Padua, Cappella degli Scrovegni.
Female clothing of the period makes all the women shown look pregnant.

6. PIERO DELLA FRANCESCA (1420-1492 approx.) *Madonna del Parto*. Monterchi, Arezzo. The dress, with the sleeves a little full at the shoulder, tight-fitting bodice with waistline slightly above the natural level and gathered skirt, was adapted to the gradual swelling of the pregnant woman's belly by slackening the laces beneath the breasts and by undoing front and side seams.

7. JAN VAN EYCK (1434 approx.) *Matrimonio Arnolfini*. The very loose-fitting hooded cloak, caught in by a belt below the breasts, is held tucked up over the stomach to allow the lady to walk and at the same time to show the garment underneath, which was often in a contrasting colour. It made all the noblewomen of Northern Europe seem well on in pregnancy.

12

6.

the dress would make it impossible for her to walk."

THE MAGISTRATE FOR CEREMONIES STEPS IN

At the beginning of the Sixteenth Century, in Venice, fashions were still well suited to dealing with the bulges of pregnancy: current wear consisted of a dress with a very short bodice, a gathered skirt and a filmy little apron. Women's clog-like shoes had now reached a very worrying height, leading the City Council to limit them to 8-9 centimeters to prevent the miscarriages caused by the frequent falls.

Cesare Vecellio informs us that in the years before his time there had been a fashion for "extraordinarily long, wide (bodices), with strips of metal inside to hold the waist in position: since it was realised that pregnant women were misusing these... the magistrate for ceremonies was forced to take action."

There are no pictures of pregnant women from this period, because no noblewoman or queen, however enlightened, has ever felt the desire to hand the image of her body rounded by pregnancy down to posterity together with those of her face, her bosom, her jewels or her rich dresses of velvet or brocade. No artist managed to persuade a pregnant woman to sit for him, even though it seems that there was no lack of immodest models available.

PREGNANCY AND PAINTERS

There is however ground for believing that, as in previous centuries, women continued to wear normal clothes, gradually slackening them as their pregnancy advanced. To prove this we have Raffaello's *La Gravida*, with the skirt and bodice of her dress divided at the normal waistline, a square neckline and a gathered apron on her stomach, in keeping with Italian fashions in the first half of the Sixteenth Century, or the woman portrayed by Moretto da Brescia in the Pietà Church in Venice, with a short corset over a white chemise and her

8. VITTORE CARPACCIO (1455-1525 approx.) *Incontro tra Orsola e Nereo*. Venice, Gallerie dell'Accademia. The tight, slashed sleeves and the gathered skirt are attached to the short bodice decorated with a plastron, by means of laces.

9. GENTILE BELLINI (1429-1507) *Il miracolo della Croce*, Venice, Gallerie dell'Accademia.
Between the end of the Fifteenth and the beginning of the Sixteenth Centuries, Venetian women wore dresses with a very short, low-cut bodice and soft, tightly gathered skirts. The slightly backwards-leaning stance puts the belly in evidence.

14

skirt and overskirt open on her swollen belly (an example of Venetian fashions of the same period).

Or Saint Anna, portrayed by Contarini just after giving birth, dressed in a bodice which comes to a slight point over her belly (typical of the second half of that Century) which is fastened only loosely. The picture in Milan cathedral of a pregnant lady at prayer, dressed in the Spanish fashion with ruff and farthingale, dates from the same period.

The farthingale, which never became fashionable in Venice, consisted of a tapered cage of steel rods and felt which lifted and pushed out the skirt. It was also known as *guardinfante* (child-protector), because, so legend would have it, it was invented by an unidentified lady "expecting a child, who was very happy to conceal her condition beneath the full shape of the farthingale." My impression is that towards the end of a pregnancy no construction on earth would be capable of masking the expectant mother's shape!

This was a period in which women were considered, without too many attempts to conceal the fact, mainly from the sexual point of view, as objects of desire and pleasure. This led to the appearance of the

10. GENTILE BELLINI (1429-1507) *La processione in Piazza S. Marco.* Venice, Gallerie dell'Accademia.
The dark overgarment (a surcoat worn over an underskirt), with its long slit at the front, concentrates all the volume on the abdomen.

11. RAFFAELLO (1483-1520) *La Gravida.* Florence, Palazzo Pitti.

16

12

13.

14.

12. GIOVANNI CONTARINI (1595 approx.) *La nascita della Vergine*. Venice, Church of the Apostles.
St Anna, in the foreground, supported by two women, has just given birth. She wears an over-garment, with the laces of the bodice loosened, over her chemise and skirt, with her shoulders covered with a "kerchief" after the fashion of the second half of the 16th Century.

13. JACOPO PALMA IL GIOVANE (1544-1628) *Madonna del Parto*. Venice, Church of St Jeremiah.
A strange picture which includes a crib, with only the baby Jesus missing. Even the swaddling bands are ready arranged on the stool. Mary wears a simple tunic in "classical" style with a belt beneath the breasts.

14. MORETTO (1498 approx.-1555 approx.) *La cena in casa del fariseo* (detail). Venice, St Mary of the Pietà.
The skirt and overskirt almost seem to lift up over the pregnant belly.

15. GEROLAMO FORABOSCO (1604-1679) *Gentildonna*. Venice. Querini Stampalia Foundation.
The dress, in fashion in the second quarter of the Seventeenth Century, is very full cut with a shrouded, almost non-existant bodice, low shoulders, full sleeves and balloon skirt. Very practical for pregnant women.

courtesans, who were intelligent, attractive, fairly well informed women with just enough culture to allow them to use their bodies to the full.

THE PANSERON AND DUTCH ROTUNDITIES

Between the end of the Sixteenth and the beginning of the Seventeenth Centuries, jackets or doublets for both men and women were padded at the front to give the idea of a prominent stomach contrasting with the slenderness of the torso itself, the perfection of the shoulders, and above all the roundness of the hips.

The full, pointed shape which emphasised the pubic region was an explicit, slightly vulgar sexual reminder. This fashion, French in origin and known as the *panseron*, seems inelegant and vulgar to our tastes, but was considered the height of eroticism during this turn of the century period, and almost replaced the obscene, much criticized

16. ALESSANDRO VAROTARI, called il Padovanino (1588-1648). *Il miracolo di una partoriente in riva al mare*, S. Giorgio di Nogaro, Cathedral.
On the right of the picture is the pregnant woman, sitting on the horse which will carry her to give birth by the sea. She wears a short bodice, huge "gigot" sleeves and a full skirt, after the fashion of the second quarter of the Seventeenth Century.

17. Ex-voto for childbirth, Naples, 16th-17th Century. Sanctuary of the Madonna of the Arch.

18. CARLO CERESA (attributed, 1609-1679). *Una gentildonna,* Venice, Querini Stampalia Foundation. Dress with just a hint of a bodice, sleeves fitting low on the shoulder and a skirt so full that it seems "puffed out."

19. SCIPIONE PULZONE (1550-1598). *Ritratto di gentildonna.* New York, Klein Collection.
The elegant zimarra opens in a suspect manner over the gown beneath, decorated in the centre with rich braiding. The gesture of the hand and the softness of the glance seem to confirm that she is pregnant.

20. FEDERICO BAROCCI (1535-1612) *Ritratto di Quintilia Fischieri.* Washington, National Gallery of Art. Kress Collection.

21. GIOVANNI GREVEMBROCH, *Gli abiti dei veneziani di quasi ogni età... dipinti nel sec. XVIII*, vol. IV c. 87.
This picture reflects the Venetians' habit of betting on everything, even on a baby's sex. A special magistrate's office was even founded to combat this habit. The pregnant woman shown wears an over-garment with fichu and loosened bodice, opening over an underskirt.

codpiece for men.

During the second quarter of the Seventeenth Century, the change in the political situation in Europe and Holland's rise in economic importance led, as usual in such circumstances, to the acceptance of fashion ideas from the new country.

Bodices became shorter again, and padded dresses and over-dresses provided fuller shapes, making the figure unusually round.

Around the middle of the century this trend underwent a further evolution, with the volumes increased even more to give the female body a decidedly "expectant woman" shape.

The dress, with a high waist, consisted of a very full, stiff skirt with a very short, filmy, gathered low-cut bodice in a very light fabric, fitting low on the shoulders.

A very full, gathered apron added to the impression of a fullblown pregnancy.

Pregnant women's problems started again with the return to tiny waists enclosed in slender bodices, during the last quarter of the Seventeenth Century.

The solution, for herself and others, was found by Madame de Montespan, Louis XIV's penultimate mistress, who did not want to appear *disgracieuse* even when pregnant and invented "a negligé which enveloped her in lace, ruches and draperies" (Contini), as practical and elegant as modern maternity wear.

FOR THE LUCKY FEW, THE ANDRIENNE

The corsets and panniers of the Eighteenth Century, a period of great male and female foolishness, made it impossible for a swollen belly to pass unobserved.

This led to the unattractive process by which the pregnant woman gradually "undid" her clothing. There are pictorial records of this: the laces of a bodice loosened over swollen breasts, skirts raised over the spherical abdomens of peasant women, or the *andriennes* or soft, flowing over-garments worn open over the all-concealing waterfalls of lace which wealthy townswomen or aristocrats were able to afford.

The elegant way round the problem for aristocratic mothers-to-be was the *andrienne*, otherwise known as the *robe à plissé Watteau* because it is illustrated abundantly and accurately in this French painter's works.

For wear over a chemise, skirt and bodice, with a bell-shaped line created by a series of deep pleats caught in on the shoulders and then allowed to fall free and full to the floor, it was invented, according to some authorities, by a famous actress, to allow her to continue to act in the play "Andrienne" by Baron in spite of her pregnancy.

22. Unknown artist of the Venetian school, second half of the 18th Century. Detail, Civici Musei, Venice.
The peasant woman, who continues spinning while listening to a Master of Ceremonies, is clearly pregnant. Her swollen belly lifts up her skirt and her apron with its decorative trim.

23. GIANDOMENICO TIEPOLO (1727-1804). *La famiglia di contadini a mensa*. Vicenza, Villa Valmarana.
The young peasant woman, who wears a colourful outfit comprising a bright blue bodice and skirt, gold kerchief, removable beige sleeves and white apron, uses her belly as a surface for resting things on, as women often do in reality.

22

24.

25.

Others maintain that its name derives from the name of Terence's comedy *Andria*, in which the actress Doncourt, who was asked to play the part of a pregnant woman, launched the fashion from the stage.

However this may be, the fact remains that in 1725 in Venice a brief book was even published (translated from the French) entitled *La famosa storia de cerchi delle donne* (The famous history of women's hoops) which claimed that the *andrienne* had been invented by a Countess Andrienne who, having fallen in love with a gallant marquis whom she was unable to marry for reasons of inheritance, hid her sinful pregnancy "beneath a tent with seven layers of hoops" which stretched her dress out to enormou sproportions. "The ladies liked this strange invention so much that the Queen herself decided to show her approval of the fashion's good taste by wearing it."

The publication also explains that the word *gard-enfant* in French means "child-protector", since women had found the hoops to be so convenient "during their indispositions, that they use them above all during their common nine months' illnesses, since in this outfit they are not under any constrictions."

IT'S DANGEROUS TO "DRAW IN YOUR WAIST"

Unfortunately, in spite of the fainting fits which resulted, women carried on wearing their corsets, completely indifferent to the physical consequences for the foetus.

In vain, the most respected obstetricians of the period thundered against the practice of "drawing in the waist" or "squeezing oneself into corsets", denouncing the shameful fact that "some women are so crazy that to make themselves look slender and tight-waisted they pull themselves in so much that they draw their whole bodies into strange shapes, meaning that after the birth they are all wrinkled like an old saddle-bag" and there could be worse consequences: all these restrictions might "prevent the child from growing correctly" or lead them to "give birth ahead of time to ill-formed babies". (Mariceau).

23

24. PIETRO LONGHI (1702-1785) *Lo svenimento*. Vicenza, Banca Cattolica del Veneto.
Fainting fits, typical of the early stages of pregnancy, were made more frequent in the Eighteenth Century by the constriction of the corset, meaning that the first aid in such cases was to loosen the clothing. The fainting woman in the picture wears only an andrienne over her chemise and skirt, as in Moreau's paintings.

25. WILLIAM HOGARTH (1697-1764). *L'attribuzione di paternità*. Dublin, National Gallery. The Eighteenth Century andrienne is covered at the front by a light apron, which should mask but in fact underlines the advanced pregnancy.

26. E. PILON, in his *La vie de famille au dix-huitième siècle*, Paris 1923. (Venice, Library of the Centro Studi di Palazzo Mocenigo, mark K 67.), reproduces three paintings by MOREAU the younger (1761-1813), which show three phases of pregnancy. The first, entitled *J'en accepte l'heureux présage*, shows the young bride looking with tears in her eyes at a baby's bonnet which her husband is showing her. The andrienne which she wears over her chemise and skirt is fastened beneath her breasts by a large bow. **26.**

27. In the second picture, entitled *Les précautions - La maternité avancée*, the lady, whose figure has thickened considerably, wears the same kind of outfit, with a fichu over her shoulders.

28. The third painting *N'ayez pas peur, ma bonne amie*, fashionable clothes adapted to her pregnancy seem bunched round her, giving her a neglected, inelegant air.

29. *La scuola di ostetricia di Verona*, 1794. List of lessons for the midwifery course.
The pregnant woman wears an "Empire" style tunic with a little shawl over her shoulders.

PREGNANCY IS IN FASHION

At the end of the Eighteenth Century, thanks not only to the Revolution but also to artistic and literary influences, fashions underwent an immense change. With the disappearance of complicated constructions and oppressive overstructures, loose, free lines were imposed and the waistline rose to just below the breast.

It is said that this style was invented by a duchess from York (no clearer identification is forthcoming) who decided to raise the waistlines of her dresses when she realised that she was expecting a baby.

Her silhouette, with upstanding breasts, full belly and large hips, was so graceful and feminine beneath the filmy fabric of her dress that even non-pregnant women decided to imitate her: it seems that they went so far as to artificially increase the size of their bellies with horsehair cushions, known as "false bellies". This drew comments from the more conservative, who stated maliciously that the fashions of that year had simply moved "the Paris bottom from the base of the spine to the abdomen" (Piantanida).

25

30. *Diderot and D'Alembert Encyclopaedia*, tab. XXIII, fig. 3. Pregnancy corset. Apart from the back and front fastenings, the corset could also be laced at the sides so that it could gradually be extended as the waistline thickened.

31. R. GAUDRIAULT. *La gravure de mode féminine en France.* Paris 1983, p. 118. The *Robe Croisée en Fichu* allowed widening of the waist, belly and hips to cope with pregnancy.

EXHORTATIONS TO "YOUNG MARRIED LADIES"

During the second quarter of the Nineteenth Century the waistline, once again very slim, returned to its natural place.

Corsets came back into fashion: they were produced in many different types which could be adapted "to all the whims of fashion" so that just "a snip of the scissors" made "the cut longer or the hips more noticeable." They were available to suit all tastes: "especially elastic for sickly or pregnant ladies", or featuring special "mechanisms" which could be undone in an instant in case of "fainting", "by just pressing one little spring".

So the exhortations of the gynaecologists, who advised ladies "to draw in the waist with moderation" to avoid miscarriages, and absolutely forbade whalebone corsets, were to no avail. One of them, Ercoliani, dedicated an entire chapter of one of his special analyses to the corset, and realizing

32.

33.

32. Model sketch from the beginning of the Nineteenth Century, with very full gathering in the skirt.

33. Two dresses, from the first half of the Nineteenth Century. The first, dating back to 1810, is Empire line while the other, dated 1840, is suitable for wear during pregnancy. Venice, Palazzo Mocenigo Museum of Costume.

34. J.P. MAYGRIER. *Nouvelles démonstrations d'accouchement*, 1822. "Toucher la femme debout" (Y. Knibiehler - C. Fouquet, *L'histoire des mères*, Paris, 1980.)
This illustration of a gynaecological examination with the woman standing up shows the patient wearing a comfortable dress with belt, after the fashion of the first quarter of the Nineteenth Century.

that it would be useless to prohibit its use during pregnancy, ruled that it could be worn "provided it adapts well to the roundness of the belly", or is drawn in only at the top "where the belly does not project".

In his view, the reason why pregnant women insisted on drawing themselves into corsets was that they did not want to have their dresses enlarged, or often "want to wear items which they have not had enlarged."

The fashion now "in fashion", which was to remain so throughout the rest of the century, imposed wasp-waists over skirts of varying fullness. This style was hostile to pregnancy, whose image it rejected as unpleasant and unseemly.

And so we should not marvel at the fact that a dress with a very stylish bodice, apparently the same as other models of the period, is indicated as appropriate for

35. *La Moda. Giornale di amena conversazione*, Venice, Tip. Commercio, 1832. Venice, Marciana National Library. The fashion sketch of the young woman standing up which appears on page 51 of the August edition is described in the explanations as showing an outfit suitable for "young wives of a few months' standing," as becomes clear if we look at the hips, which "are rather larger than normal".

36. SILVESTRO LEGA (1826-1895). *Passeggiata.*
This picture, which can be dated to around 1860-65 because of the width of the crinoline, shows a young pregnant woman talking to a friend. The pregnancy is suggested by the shape of the skirt and of the short, bag-shaped jacket.

28

37. *Margherita. Giornale delle signore italiane,* April 1880. The typical pose of a woman who fainted because of pregnancy.

"brides of a few months' standing" whose hips (the description adds) "if we look at them carefully, are perhaps slightly larger than usual." This shy euphemism and absurd footnote were intended to allude to pregnancy.

In fact all the women's magazines, of which there were now many for all levels of society, used the phrase "young married lady", or "young wife" to refer to pregnancy, in view of the young age at which women usually bore children.

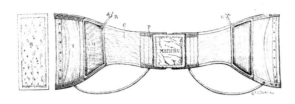

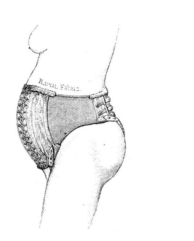

DRESSES FOR CHILDBIRTH

Luckily for those poor ladies, in 1838 they were already being offered coats with very full lines, shoulder capes, cloaks and large shawls in which they could wrap themselves outside the home to conceal their embarrassing bulges.

An interesting, but little-known fact is the existance in that period of "childbirth dresses", described in an important midwifery textbook of 1840 as follows: "shirt reaching down to the hips and a full skirt opening at the side, with laces or ribbons opening on the hips." This allowed the doctor to follow the birth while remaining at the side of the woman in labour.

Thumbing through the women's magazines of the second half of the Nineteenth Century, which now had a fairly large circulation, it is impossible to understand their complete silence on this subject: after all, they were catering for a basically female readership and tackled a wide variety of both frivolous and practical subjects.

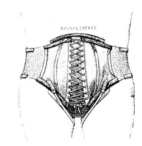

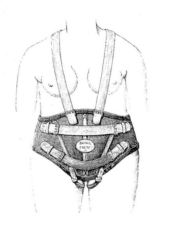

38. G.J. WITKOWKSI, *Histoire des accouchements chez tous les peuples*, Paris, 1887, pp 910-911. Venice, Library of the Ospedale Civile SS. Giovanni e Paolo.
While medical texts of this period complained against the use of the corset during pregnancy, this book provided precise details of the kind of corset suitable for supporting the muscles of the maternal belly.

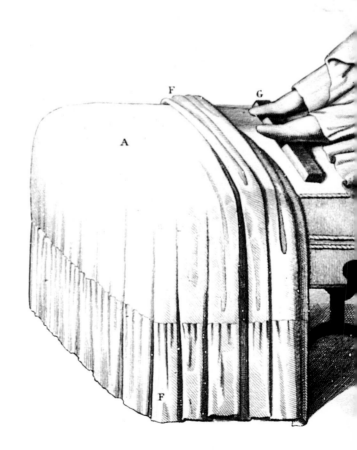

30

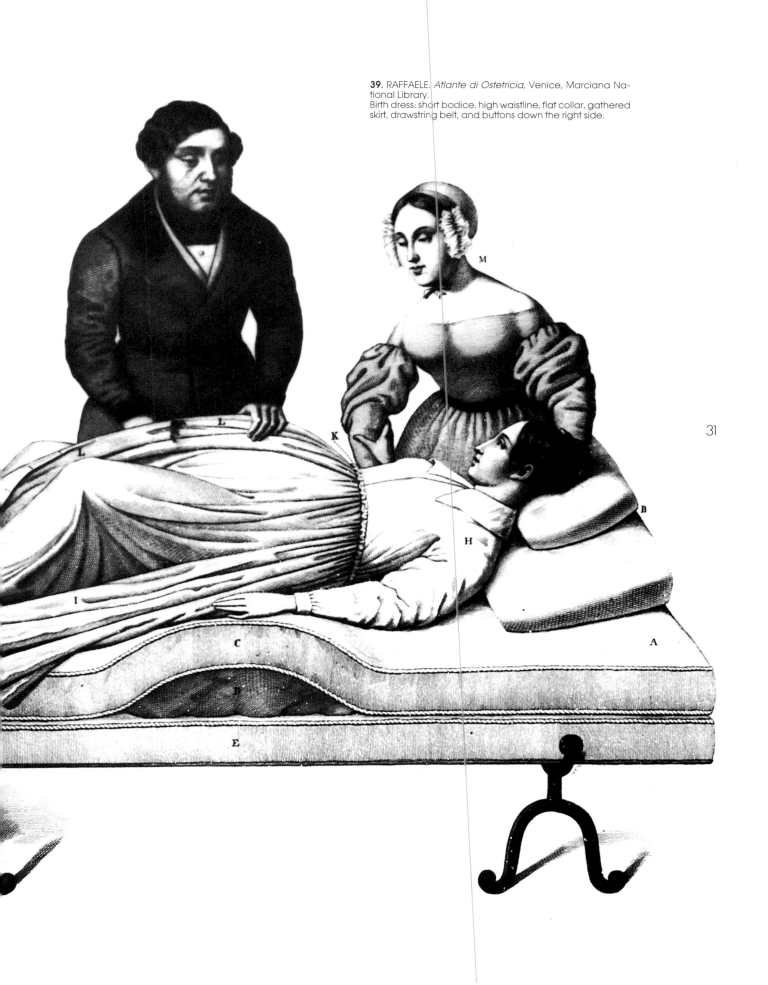

39. RAFFAELE. *Atlante di Ostetricia*, Venice, Marciana National Library.
Birth dress: short bodice, high waistline, flat collar, gathered skirt, drawstring belt, and buttons down the right side.

In *Natura ed Arte* in 1984, a "historical" article explained that "the hooped skirt was invented by Eugenia to conceal the fact that the poor little prince was about to be born," and this fashion was immediately followed by "Queen Victoria, who on her side was about to give birth to Princess Beatrice". If even the queens themselves were ashamed of their pregnancies, hiding them beneath crinolines and illustrating the unease and distaste with which they endured a condition not accepted by society, it is clear that their behaviour would be followed and imitated by the great mass of women.

WORTH AND THE.... ENCEINTES

A recent, but well researched historical novel on the couturier Worth tells that when one of his staff became pregnant "she made herself a few short jackets trimmed with bows, similar in fashion to those which he (the great couturier) had designed for his wife Marie when she was expecting a child."

These garments were very effective in concealing the thickening of the body around the waistline "and they were so elegant that Worth received many orders, even from customers who were not *enceintes*. When the *mannequin's* condition became so obvious that it was impossible to conceal it, Worth asked her to model his "maternity creations" in a room open only to ladies in her own "advanced state", with her face covered by a veil "to avoid any embarrassment." (Laker).

The papers continued to discuss "*chemises* for daywear for young married ladies", or dresses "suitable for married ladies, in view of the special considerations of the changes of state to which young married ladies may be subject", or garments which were "very convenient in certain special circumstances", all referring to full, loose-fitting styles with little folds and furbelows on the front.

40. *La Moda*. Milan, Treves, 1887, p. 147
Of the three jackets shown, while two follow the dictates of current fashions, the first on the left seems to be intended for the mother to be.

32

41. *Il Monitore della Moda*, Milan, December 1st, 1886, p.2. Flared "visiting costume". The masking fringe decoration looks as though it might even have been designed by Worth.

42. *Il Monitore della Moda*, Milan, December 1st, 1886, p.4 Hooded dress. The folds and clustered pleats on the front must be to suit the expectant mother.

43. England (1858-1860). Pregnancy outfit of the Victorian era in taffetta, in the "princess" style. Widens towards the hemline as the darts on the bodice open out.

44. *La Stagione, Giornale delle Dame*, Milan, June 1st 1888, n. 17. Here again there are two solutions available: the blouse on the right is obviously intended for maternity wear.

33

34

45. *La Moda.* Milan, Treves 1889. Venice, Querini Stampalia Library. The young woman in the centre is wearing a dress which would allow for gradual thickening of the figure. Women's magazines provided suggestions without putting them into words.

THE BELLA EPOQUE

FASHIONS FOR THE "PLUMP"

At the turn of the century, the Art Nouveau or Liberty movement, born from the genius of William Morris and the "Arts and Crafts" movement, succeeded in drawing even the fashion world into its sphere of influence, offering a loose-fitting, practical line with no constrictions which was also very feminine.

The same period saw the revival of the "Empire line" dress, which became more and more popular in spite of the continuation in fashion of the "S" shape, with its ridiculous equilibrium between the curves of the bosom and the bottom.

The magazines emphasize that the "Liberty" style dresses seemed to be designed especially for expectant mothers, or, in vaguer terms, for the "plump", who wore them to avoid the criticisms of their friends who have nothing better to do than to "measure the too-large waistline with their eyes."

THE REFORM DRESS

It was at the beginning of the Twentieth Century that the Reform dress became to appear more and more frequently, at first only in the intimacy of the home, but later also in society. Basically similar to the "Empire" dress, it was welcomed as a conquest and a well-deserved reward for

46. Anonymous designer of the beginning of the Twentieth Century. Full, oriental type dress in fashion according to the dictates of the Liberty style. It was the end of the corset.

women. "Only in our age has the consciousness of incongruities come to maturity in our feminine world, causing for the first time the birth of a movement for the reformation of women's clothing."

Born in Germany, this movement "has nothing to do with fashion, but is inspired only by rational considerations and the principles of hygiene," directing its attention first and foremost against the corset, instead of which it offered "elegant bands" in classical style.

And so articles on corsets were very newsworthy, appearing more and more frequently in women's magazines. In 1901 a "Dott. Antonio" dedicated two long editions of his weekly column in *Margherita* to this article, giving an outline of its prehistory (from the Roman *fasciae mamillares*) and history, with one or two unusual pieces of information regarding the Nineteenth Century, and finishing by recommending a corset with wide "side bands of elastic material" to "all pregnant ladies."

On the same subject, Rossi Doria, a famous obstetrician of the time, stated that

36

48.

47.

49.

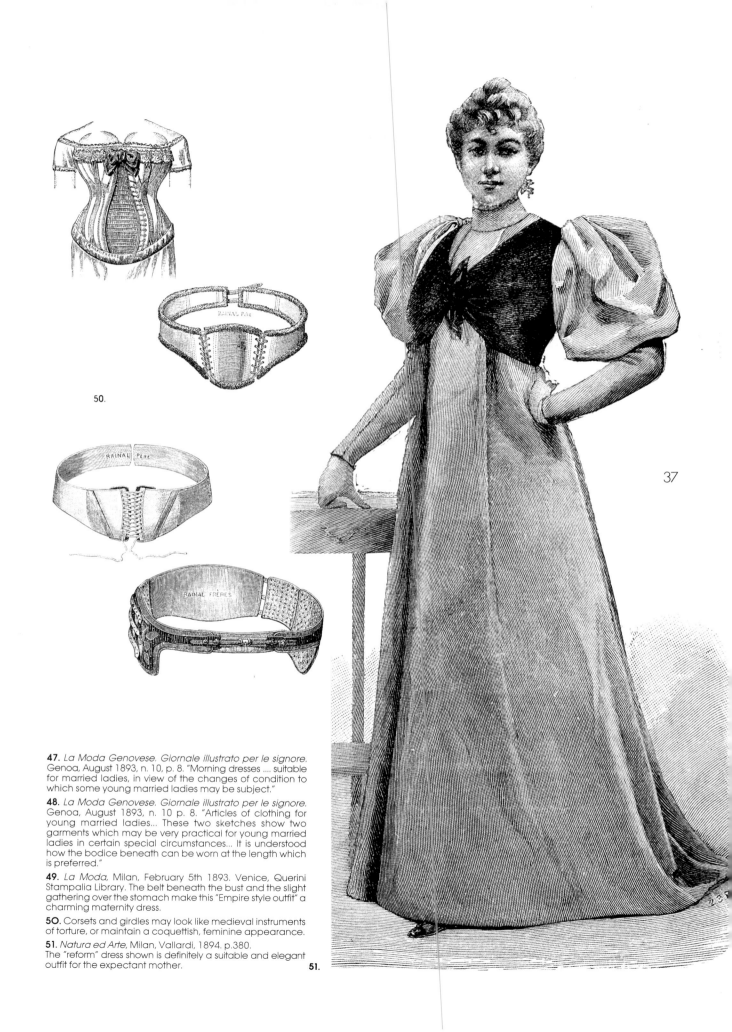

47. *La Moda Genovese. Giornale illustrato per le signore.* Genoa, August 1893, n. 10, p. 8. "Morning dresses .... suitable for married ladies, in view of the changes of condition to which some young married ladies may be subject."

48. *La Moda Genovese. Giornale illustrato per le signore.* Genoa, August 1893, n. 10 p. 8. "Articles of clothing for young married ladies... These two sketches show two garments which may be very practical for young married ladies in certain special circumstances... It is understood how the bodice beneath can be worn at the length which is preferred."

49. *La Moda*, Milan, February 5th 1893. Venice, Querini Stampalia Library. The belt beneath the bust and the slight gathering over the stomach make this "Empire style outfit" a charming maternity dress.

50. Corsets and girdles may look like medieval instruments of torture, or maintain a coquettish, feminine appearance.

51. *Natura ed Arte*, Milan, Vallardi, 1894. p.380. The "reform" dress shown is definitely a suitable and elegant outfit for the expectant mother.

50.

37

51.

"the corsets which are now in fashion, which raise the belly instead of pressing it down like those used in the past, tend to be beneficial to the pregnancy."

PROPOSALS AND SOLUTIONS

But let's get back to clothes. A practical manual for dressmakers states, in the short chapter dedicated to "dresses for young married ladies" that it must be easy to widen and lengthen these to adapt them at any time to follow the changes in the body's shape right down to the birth of the baby. Hints and ideas are provided for the

52. *Natura ed Arte*, Milan, 1902 (A. XI-I s) pp 83-87.
"House dress for afternoon tea, very elegant and simple. Empire style..."

53. Photograph of a family group, Milan, autumn 1899. (Casarsa, Pellissetti Archive.)
The young lady sitting in the foreground with the white gloves is well gone in pregnancy (she was to give birth in January 1900). Beneath her dark cloak, she wears a simple blouse and skirt.

38

54.

54. *Natura ed Arte*. Milan, 1908 (A. XI-I s)pp 83-87.
To adapt this design with Liberty style decoration to the
fuller figure, all one had to do was to move the side buttons.
The dressing-gown was recommended to young married
ladies because of its loose, comfortable line.

55. Maternity dress, Veneto, 19th-20th Century. (Venice,
Centro Studi di Storia del Costume e del Tessuto, Palazzo
Mocenigo.)

55.

56. G. KLIMT, *L'Espoir,* 1903. Oil on canvas, 181 x 67. National Gallery, Ottawa.

57. D. BACCARINI (1883-1907). *Giovinetta incinta* 1904. A serene image of the mother-to-be.

58. H. TOULOUSE-LAUTREC. *Madame Abdala.* Woodcut, (L.D. 33). Cruelly realistic portrayal by the artist of the Moulin Rouge when the Belle Epoque was at its height.

gradual adaptation of skirts and bodices, which are easy to extend: "it is sufficient to just slacken the ribbon fastening," as women had been doing for centuries.

The Eighteenth Century "panniers" also made a comeback, used to drape the skirt "with elegance" to form two light concave bumps on the hips, while the belief that "the Reform dress is the best solution for every pregnant lady" was increasingly repeated by commentators, since women had now widely adopted this style with its high waistline and long, flowing skirt. However, in the few photograph portraits which have come down to us (these are rare since there was a widspread superstition that having one's photograph taken during pregnancy was bad for the child) the pregnant ladies continue to wear skirts and blouses.

Even Bitta, the young mistress of the painter Baccarini, portrayed during her

59. *Regina*, Milan, March 30th 1905 n. 3 page 25. (Venice, Ieri Attualità Archive.) Tina di Lorenzo, actress and mother, symbol of regal, vital beauty, wears a "Liberty" dress decorated with bobbin lace, which does not hide the fact that she is pregnant.

60. *Natura ed Arte*. Milan, 1903. (A. XI-II s.) p. 91 "Two outfits for the young married lady, one in black *péluche* with jacket loose-fitting at the front, with vertical seams, and very full sleeves ..... smooth skirt."

61.64. *La mode pratique*, February 1906. (Venice, Ieri Attualità Archive). Some examples of coats, suits and dresses for afternoon wear unmistakable designed for the expectant mother.

60.

61.

62.

63.

64.

pregnancy, wore simply a skirt and blouse buttoned on the left, with a short gathered basque.

POIRET AND THE HIGH-WAISTED JACKET

All references to fashions inspired by flowers were now slowly disappearing, and the changes in lines and tastes were noticeable at all levels in society.

65-66. *La mode pratique* February 1906. (Venice, Ieri Attualità Archive.)

67. A. WITTE. *La sarta moderna*, Milan.

68. A. WITTE. *La sarta moderna*, Milan. The dress recommended for the pregnant lady has a pleated bodice with a lace cascade on the front, and a skirt with elastic at the waist and an uneven hemline.

69. A. WITTE. *La sarta moderna*, Milan. A few examples of skirts and bodices which can be modified during pregnancy.

70. Photograph of a family and servants, Venice 1910. (Toso Murano Archive, reproduced by F. Turio). The second young woman from the right in the front row, sitting down (who is known to have been pregnant at the time) wears a very simple, practical, attractive trapezium-shaped overblouse over her dress.

71. D. BACCARINI (1883-1907) *Il corredino.*

Alongside tunics of different lengths worn one over the other in "pagoda" fashion, the first tailored suits, with a rather severe air and a little padding on the shoulders, began to appear.

Poiret, the new star of the Paris fashion world, held a highly theatrical party in "Thousand and one nights" style to launch the image of the odalisque woman, perfumed and luxurious and generally lightly clad. One dress in particular was welcomed with enthusiasm everywhere: "a high-

72. CHARLES MARTIN, *Robe d'interieur*, 1911.

73. *Journal des dames et des modes*, Paris, 20 avril 1913, n. 33. Dark blue satin, white tulle and black and white "de Chine" brocade feature in an evening creation which is extremely feminine thanks to its implicit reference to the pregnant form: the curved line which dominates seems to flow onto and out from the stomach.

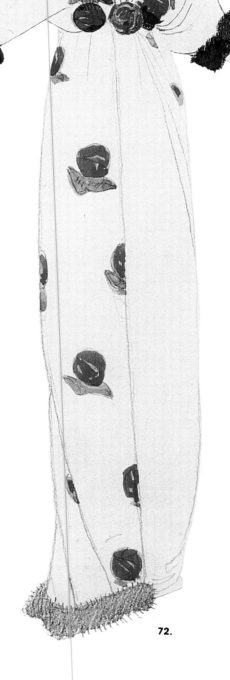

47

73.

72.

74.

J. van Brock.

76.

75.

74. *Journal des dames et des modes*, Paris, December 1st 1912. The flowing line of the pre-war years, practical and sophisticated, was also very suitable for pregnancy.

75. *Journal des dames et des modes*, Paris, dédié a l'occasion du 1 Janvier 1913. The four Poiret-style models, designed by Martin, are the most amusing, cheerful and elegant designs one could imagine for a woman, even during pregnancy.

76. *Journal des dames et des modes*, Paris, 10 avril 1914, n. 68. The large tapered plissé flounce, an original and bizarre invention, makes a strong reference to pregnancy by widening the hips and belly.

77.78. GEORGES BARBIER. *Chez Poiret* 1911. Designs with high, unmarked waistline.

77.

78.

waisted jacket with a little basque drawn in with a cord.... slightly gathered skirt."

The vertical line of the designs and the compulsory abandonment of the corset and "all that complex of underwear consisting of knickers and petticoats required by the modesty of the Nineteenth Century" (Butazzi) emphasized the body's suppleness.

Furthermore, perhaps as a result of the first women's congresses held more or less all over Europe, even in Italy, and because of the healthy trend towards an increase in sporting activity, some daring tailors risked launching the *jupe-culotte*, which however was worn only by the most open-minded and by the most daring ladies of all: the pilots.

79. V.V.A.A. *Paul Poiret et Nicole Groult*, Paris, Palais Galliera 1986.
The high-waisted skirt and overskirt make this model, worn by NICOLE GROULT in 1916, suitable for pregnancy.

80. Photograph of a pregnant lady, Venice, 1914. (Uberti-Raccanelli Archive, reproduction by F. Turio). The walking-out coat, with its straight cut and button fastening on the left hand side, is quite elegant but not appropriate for the expectant mother.

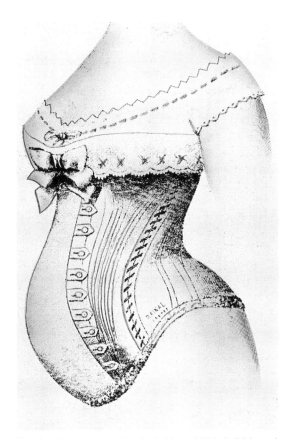

81. H. SPEERT, *Iconographia Gyniatrica - A Pictorial History of Gynecology and Obstetrics.* Philadelphia, 1973. The corset shown, dating from the last quarter of the 19th Century, supports the pregnant woman's belly very well while still being attractive to look at.

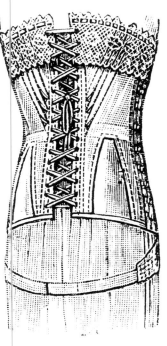

82. Photograph of a pregnant lady. Venice 1914. (Uberti-Raccanelli Archive, reproduction by F. Turio). The very full blouse attractively reflects the thickened figure.

83. *Il Ricamo*, Milan, July 18th 1915, n. 29. "Corset for young married ladies. Very practical thanks to the new supporting shape which it incorporates."

52

AFTER THE WAR
THE ROARING TWENTIES

THE NEW HORIZONS

Cutting back on expenses was so absolutely "respectable" in the years immediately following the First World War, and the feeling of impoverishment was so widespread, that the effect of this tendence is immediately obvious in the clothes of the period, both in the savings on the materials used and in the limited choice of colours available.

The emancipation of women progressed rapidly in the Western world in general following the concrete, active role they had played in the war itself, but this development did not take place in Italy. A new, industrialized world with new production methods was taking shape, bringing about a far-reaching transformation in women's lives. They became more and more eager to shake off their centuries-old role as dolls and to affirm their own personalities, their intelligence and their right to legal, social and political equality.

The protagonists in the Roaring Twenties, women obtained the vote in England in 1918, in most of Europe in 1919 and in the United States of America in 1920.

Fashions changed completely: the corsets and tight-waisted jackets which emphasized the bosom and hips disappeared, and women cut their hair *à la garçonne* and wore "short, basic tube dresses which slipped over their bodies without altering their

84. V.V.A.A. *Paul Poiret et Nicole Groult.* Paris, Palais Galliera, 1986. *Un mannequin dans le jardin de Poiret vers le 1922.* Skirt with flared jacket: a design for the mother to be?

85. Group photograph, Padua 1926. (Buzzaccarini Archive, photograph by Gislon). The fourth lady from the left, who is pregnant (verbal testimony), wears an elegant straight coat.

shape, with belts worn low on the hips to underline their slenderness." (Masucci).

DONNA CLARA AND HER ADVICE FOR LADIES

In Italy, on the other hand, Fascism sent women back to household tasks and ignorance: excluded from office jobs and from the schools, they were banned from teaching literature and philosophy in the grammar schools and made to pay double for university tuition.

What mattered was producing children, because "numbers mean power".

All the same, pregnancy continued to be a long dark period, the last months of which were spent withdrawn from society. Donna Clara, the arbiter of elegance of the age, advised "young married ladies" to dress "so that no item of clothing is pressing against the body" and "above all so as to attract as little attention as possible."

To underline her point, she added:

"One would think that all mothers would feel the same amount of protective modesty about their condition; but we come across women who seem completely unaffected by this sensation: they exhibit their shape shamelessly and wear eye-catching clothes. For heaven's sake!" she concludes, "everyone should wear simple, loose-fitting clothes, with nothing tight or showy."

The thing which women themselves disliked up to not so many years ago was the implicit idea of the "sinful" act required to produce a pregnant belly. This idea led even midwives to come out with sentences such as "You've had your fun and now you have to suffer for it," during labour, linking a biblical sense of guilt to the most natural event in the world.

But that is not all. In fact, there's an anecdote that someone even once heard a young woman exclaim, in an evident Freudian slip, "...I can't stand pregnant women either. They wave their bellies in your face as if to say: I've made love and you have not."

MORE COMFORTABLE BY
FORCE OF CIRCUMSTANCES

The year 1913 confirmed the advance of a style of fashion which was, in general, comfortable: diamond-shaped coats full on the hips and tight at the ankles worn over dresses in the same style, making the enchantress who wore them look like a kind of mysterious moth.

This line, with an almost maternity cut, alternated with others which could, with a little imagination, be described as the "skittle" or "aubergine" styles.

To tell the truth, in these garments women looked not so much dressed as wrapped up, even though the quality of the materials used and the languid postures adopted created a very chic, sophisticated effect.

By force of circumstances, the Great War put an end to this image of luxurious femininity, bringing new, astonishingly modern elements into fashions.

The flow of female labour into many sectors (even heavy industry, which had previously been reserved for men) caused by the departure of the menfolk for the front, forced women to abandon their skirts in favour of trousers (and this sometimes happened even in Italy), or in any case obliged them to shorten their dresses to make them suitable for all movements and all tasks.*

* For bibliography and source documents on this subject for the period considered so far see: D. DAVANZO POLI: "L'abbigliamento in gravidanza, parto e puerperio" in AA.VV. *Nascere a Venezia*, Torino 1985, pp 55-79 and catalogue cards.

86. *La Mode Illustrée*, Paris, 1920 (Venice, Library of the Centro Studi di Palazzo Mocenigo). The "aubergine" line coats and jackets were well suited to pregnancies, which were still considered somewhat embarrassing.

56

87.

FROM THE FABULOUS THIRTIES...
TWENTY YEARS OF RESIGNATION

MALE CHAUVINISM AND
DEMOGRAPHIC CONCERNS

With its campaign to increase the birth
rate, Fascism impoverished the human
and social aspects of women's lives and, by
encouraging a long series of enforced
pregnancies, emphasized their role as
mothers to the detriment of everything
else. The fashions of the time, which
tried to compensate for poor quality fabrics
with daring inventions and new ideas in
tailoring, were unable to offer garments
exclusively for the expectant mother.

On this subject, in 1937 the Ente Na-
zionale della Moda (National Fashion
Organization) put Italian women on
their guard about the negative influence
which clothes could have on their desire
to have children, stating that foreign
fashions tended to lead female thoughts
in the wrong direction, giving women an
image which was "attractive, youthful,
desirable, but not that of a mother." It
therefore advised the female sex to leave
such worthless fripperies "to women
whose childbearing lives are over."

If at the bourgeois social level efforts
were made to hinder female emancipation,
women were accepted and much in demand

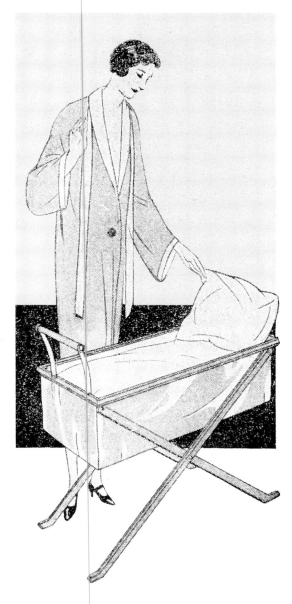

57

87. *Femina.* Paris, October 1932, special issue, p. 7 (Venice,
Ieri Attualità Archive).
The black velvet evening cape with ermine collar and cuffs,
square shoulders, flared cut and just a hint of a sleeve is
ideal for a sophisticated mother-to-be.

88. One can tell that this loose-fitting dress is intended for
the expectant mother, especially if it is illustrated next to a
cot. Around 1930.

88.

as manual workers. It made economic sense to employ them in the factories, since the Fascist trade unions had lowered their wages to half the corrisponding rates for men.

And so it was only to be expected that women came to consider their femininity as an obstacle to their self-realization, and tried to play it down, rejecting the hated canons of classical beauty. Lines therefore became more masculine, with the bosom and hips flattened and the shoulders becoming wider, padded and square in shape.

The "regime" responded to this provocation by imposing an image of a shapely, bold woman, the young lady called *signorina grandi firme*.

90.

58

89.

89. *Le Jardin des Modes.* Paris, March 15th 1936. (Venice, Ieri Attualità Archive)
Strong colour contrasts and tightly gathered "painter's smocks" are in fashion.

90. *Le Jardin des Modes*, Paris, March 15th 1936. (Venice, Ieri Attualità Archive).
Other full-cut jacket styles which open out from the shoulders, with raglan sleeves.

91.   92.   93.   94.

91. *Dea*, Milan, April 1937 n. 4. "In attesa del bimbo". (Venice, Ieri Attualità Archive)
"A few very practical, elegant *Dea* patterns for the lady who is expecting a baby. Three-quarter skirt in dark blue wool crepe.... Very flared jacket for wear in the morning or early afternoon, in untreated rayon cloth."

92. *Dea,* Milan. April 1937 n. 4 "In attesa del bimbo". (Venice, Ieri Attualità Archive).
"Flared three quarters jacket in black and natural green tartan lanital. Large yoke beneath which the fairly wide sleeves are attached."

93. *Dea,* Milan, April 1937 n. 4 "In attesa del bimbo". (Venice, Ieri Attualità Archive).
"Black cape in light wool and cotton cloth. The back is made loose-fitting by a central panel"... Black silk crepe dress. The skirt is made fuller-fitting by pleats, the bodice is fairly loose and the sleeves have round shoulder. Bright coloured neck-scarf."

94. *Dea,* Milan, April 1937 n. 4 "In attesa del bimbo". (Venice, Ieri Attualità Archive).
"Cape-dress in heavy synthetic fibre crepe in a natural shade. The dress is cut straight, with just a gather which forms pleats on the front..."

95. *Dea,* Milan, April 1937 n. 4 "In attesa del bimbo". (Venice, Ieri Attualità Archive).
"Dress in rayon with printed pattern on dark background, pleated throughout..." The model shown is really unusual as maternity wear, although one can see how the pleats would adapt to the thickening of the figure.

96. *Dea,* Milan, April 1937 n. 4 "In attesa del bimbo." (Venice, Ieri Attualità Archive).
"Very elegant evening dress. The skirt is in pale blue rayon crepe, flared towards the hem.... The short tunic is in bright blue sequins and is cut in a single piece. Lace flowers."

95.

96.

Looking through the few glossy magazines which have survived from the Thirties (most of them were transformed, by soaking and pressing into balls, into a cheap fuel during the Second World War), it is noticeable yet again that all the questions related to female life were dealt with, from problems of hygiene to aesthetic considerations, without pregnancy and birth ever being mentioned.

Advice was given on healthy, productive leisure occupations (such as, for example, the creation of an embroidered cushion "to give to your husband so that he can rest his tired feet on it when he comes home from work") and trite romantic fiction was serialized, while real problems were avoided altogether.

However, from the history of clothing point of view the feature on fashion for mothers-to-be which appeared in the magazine *Dea* in 1937, directed at women of a medium-high economic class, was important.

These were sketches of very original designs, which tried out new ideas, while of course using some formulas dictated by necessity. There was nothing really spectacular: gathered overshirts and tunics in striped or brightly checked fabric, which still hesitated to describe themselves honestly as truly "maternity". In a period of history where everything English and American was censored, it would be useless to hope that the progressive feminine ideas developing in those countries might be allowed to filter through.

97. Maria-Josè, Princess of Piedmont, was always unconventional. This was confirmed by the fact that she allowed herself to be photographed not only pregnant, but also in a bathing costume. (The photograph appeared in an old edition of "Oggi").

98. *Fili,* Milan 1941, n. 12 pp 46-47 (Library of th Centro Studi di Palazzo Mocenigo).
Masquerading as dresses for the house or the office, these are really for maternity wear.

97.

INFLUENCES FROM AFAR

During the period immediately following the conflict which has gone down in history as the Second World War, the latest novelties on the maternity fashion scene reached Europe together with the boogie-woogie, chewing-gum and coca-cola. In the meantime, women in Italy had acquired the vote, no less than twenty-two of them had been elected to the Constituent Assembly, and they were starting to show their dissatisfaction with the old man-woman relationship within the family with all the decision-making and authority on the one side and nothing but submission and dependence on the other.

99. *Maternity Dresses, Maternity Sportswear.* SEARS catalogue, New York 1949. (Bertarelli Print Collection, Milan). While in Italy maternity clothing was still left to the individual, the United States were already offering real maternity dresses illustrated in the mail-order catalogues. (Photographs by Saporetti.)

63

Dior launched the new look, bringing
back the image of the doll-like, fragile,
sophisticated, wealthy woman with her
waist drawn in by whaleboned corsets and
her hips widened by a crinoline.

The pregnant woman (the Italian word
is "incinta", from the Latin *in-cincta*, meaning "without a belt") was to continue to
keep her new-found dignity intact.

100.101. *Jardin des Modes*, avril-décembre 1949 n. 328
p. 49; n. 336 pp 37 and 40 (Venice, Ieri Attualità Archive).
FATH, GRIFFE and MOLYNEUX offer full, loose-fitting capes
for all occasions.

102. BRUYÈRE and BALMAIN look to the Far East for clothes
for Western pregnancies.

101.

100.

102.

103. *Harper's Bazaar* July 1949 n. 2739 p. 35 (Venice, Ieri Attualità Archive). Schiaparelli lunch outfit consisting of smooth tunic dress and bag-shaped jacket.

EVERYTHING'S NEW, EVEN KITSCH

CLOTHES FROM YOUR
FAVOURITE DRESSMAKER

During the euphoric Fifties, the years of reconstruction and hard work aimed at overcoming the bad times left behind, people wanted an image of wasteful luxury to allow them to show everyone the wealth they had acquired.

After all, the more the better.

Becoming the symbol of the decade, larger sized ladies exaggerated their already abundant shapes by wearing dresses covered in frills, flounces, drapes and plissé.

It was a triumph for bad taste and vulgarity, but the road to progress was open and people carried on along it regardless.

In Italy, between the end of the Forties and the beginning of the new decade, "maternity wear" was still not widely available: the most practical garments for this purpose were recommended to customers by dressmakers, or inherited from more experienced sisters or friends. The best-known pattern was a dress with cross-over bodice and a skirt with wrap-over front fastening: the large amount of fabric inevitably required was held in by a drawstring belt at the waist, which was

104. *Annabella*, Milan, 1956, n. 49 (Venice, Ieri Attualità Archive). The Princess of Monaco, in ordinary life Grace Kelly, the Hollywood star, does not give up her excellent social life just because she is expecting a baby.

Ne aveva sentito parlare...

Il commendatore: — Ma sarà poi vero che questo sistema psicoprofilattico elimina la pancia senza dolore?

Caro Attalo,
grazie per questa vignetta con la quale hai voluto prendere in giro il nostro film

105. *La Settimana Incom.* Milan 1957 n. 10 p. 35. (Venice, Ieri Attualità Archive).
Humourous cartoon on the subject of painless childbirth, referring to the film *Il momento più bello* with Marcello Mastroianni and Giovanna Ralli.

106. *La Settimana Incom.* Rome 1956 n. 3 pp. 60-61 (Venice, Ieri Attualità Archive).
Expectant mothers prepare for the birth by doing exercises, for which they wear trousers and T-shirts.

107. *Mode Charmante*, Florence, 1951. (Venice, Library of the Centro Studi di Palazzo Mocenigo).
Various styles of full-cut jacket (with some ideas already seen in previous years) very appropriate for a modern pregnancy.

106.

107.

gradually loosened as the pregnancy advanced. The colours were fairly dull and powdery: for daytime there was a choice between grey and dark blue, while bright blue was acceptable for the summertime and for very young mothers-to-be. The pregnant "socialite" always adopted the black "wrap-over" dress for evening wear. The fabric had of course to be soft and flowing, so wool crepes, jersey and heavy handle pure or mixed silk crepe de chine were the favourites (de Buzzaccarini).

In the mid - Fifties the *Settimana Incom*, well known because of the cinema magazine of the same name, dedicated a long article to childbirth "without fears", informing its readers that "pain is not necessary in childbirth": if this fact had already been "affirmed by medical science for some time", it was now recognised "even by Catholic morality", this last being an unmistakable reference to the reflections on the subject by Pope Pius XII at the beginning of 1956.

The pages of the same magazine showed the smiling face of a very young Ira Fürstenberg, heavily pregnant, beside her aristocratic husband.

NEW PROFESSIONS FOR DYNAMIC WOMEN

In 1957, *Così*, one of the most sophisticated, pretentious women's weekly magazines of the period, presented a long feature on "Elegance for mothers-to-be."

A self-justifying introduction explained that, "The period before the birth of a child is definitely the most wonderful period of a woman's life, when her grace becomes more spiritual and all her habits are regulated by a protective, tender defence of her own body. Even her way of dressing is inspired by more practical

108.

109.

108. *Gioia*, Milan, 1956, n. 26. A grey shantung suit with little flared jacket. The tube skirt has two adjustable darts at the waist.

109. *La Settimana Incom*. Rome, 1956. n. 46 p. 53. (Venice, "Ieri Attualità" Archive).
A very young, very famous expectant mother, Ira von Fürstenberg, wearing dull, severe clothes to pass unnoticed.

70

110. *Gioia*, Milan, 1956, n. 26. The straight skirt and sleeveless jacket with round neck in cool wool give a demure air.

111. *Così*, Milan, January 13th 1957. (Venice, Ieri Attualità Archive).
"For expectant mothers. Shirt-dress in almond green jersey follows the figure without clinging too much. Note the side fastening which may be gradually shifted...." (Manguin).

112. *Gioia*, Milan, 1956, n. 26. Pleats are always up to date for maternity dresses for elegant occasions. If it's in silk organza delicate shades are preferable.

113. *Così*, Milan, January 13th 1957. (Venice, Ieri Attualità Archive).
"For mothers-to-be, the interesting feature of this dress are the pleats in the skirt, specially designed to accommodate the modifications required by the expectant mother. The shirt has two adjustable pleats, and the bodice is also adjustable."

114. *Così*, Milan, January 13th 1957. (Venice, Ieri Attualità Archive).
"Elegance for the expectant mother. The flannel dress is particularly suitable for the mother-to-be because.... it is highly practical. The outfit is designed so that the bodice can be replaced with a practical jacket with full pleats on the front."

112.   **113.**   **114.**

considerations, cutting out irrational fashions and ridiculous constrictions in favour of dresses with flowing lines which fall softly around the figure, seeming to defend a precious secret which is not exactly concealed, but which requires that modest grace dear to every gentle soul."

There is a new spirit in these words, even if they are aimed at restraining the strong feeling of power which every pregnant woman feels, which would naturally lead her to show off her fertility. The styles illustrated in this article are very classy, with inspired design ideas which are so timeless that they are still used unchanged today. After all, it was during these very Fifties that Italian women were allowed

115. *Gioia*, Milan, 1956, n. 56. Blouse in sky-blue, ivory white or pink poplin. The choice of colour depends on the concept of *bon ton* which was still generally accepted at the time.

116. *Gioia*, Milan, 1956, n. 26. The evergreen tunic with box-pleats in silk twill is an elegant number for a comfortable pregnancy.

115.

116.

117. *Eva*, Milan, May 17th 1958 p. 4 (Venice, Ieri Attualità Archive).
The white collar, the bow and the flower are all details which give an idea of innocence and spiritual purity. "Baby doll" princess dress in coarse navy blue fabric with large round collar in white piquet. The flat bow is also in piquet.

118. *La Settimana Incom*. Milan, 1958 n. 5 (Venice, Ieri Attualità Archive).

119. *La Linea*, Milan, 1957 n. 76 p. 92 (Venice, Library of the CSTC Palazzo Mocenigo).
The trapezium shape, launched by Dior and Yves Saint Laurent, is a step forward for women, especially those expecting a baby.

117.

118.

access to new professions thanks to the growth of made in Italy fashions, thanks to the development of the sales networks of companies which had so far operated only on a small scale, public relations, and the expansion of journalism for the specialist women's and fashion press. Working women don't abandon their offices just because they are pregnant, but they need clothing which suits a more streamlined lifestyle. The smoke-grey heavy flannel suit from London which suited their requirements had a double-breasted jacket with military collar and a cleverly fitted cut. The matching skirt was straight cut with a little kick-pleat in the centre back and a big "hole" in the front to leave space for the enlarged belly (de Buzzaccarini)

In this atmosphere, with its emphasis on the cultural rediscovery of motherhood

120.121. *Linea*, Milan, 1957 n. 76 (Venice, Library of the CSTC Palazzo Mocenigo). The new trapezium or sack shape with open darts beneath the bust is very suitable for an attractive maternity style.

and of the new lifestyle requirements of the mother-to-be, Yves Saint Laurent, a new designer, Dior's heir and pupil, launched the trapezium line dress, featuring narrow shoulders and a full hemline. This was a milestone in the history of women's clothing, and, surprise, surprise! clearly suitable for use as maternity wear.

PRESS FEATURES ON ....
FAMOUS BELLIES

The women we've just been considering, who did not passively submit to events but took part in them, allowing themselves to be caught up in social changes and freeing themselves from the old schemes of thought to mature new values, found that they were able to realize themselves more fully outside the home.

The consolidation of peace and stable economic well-being for almost everyone made both men and women more tolerant and secure. And journals could take the liberty of dedicating a lengthy feature to a

122.123. *Novità*, Milan, March 1955 n. 53 p. 42 (Venice, Ieri Attualità Archive.)
J. VENEZIANI and G. MARUCELLI offer very elegant outfits for the mother-to-be.

124.

125.

124. *Così*, Milano, 13 gennaio 1957. (Venice, Ieri Attualità Archive.) "The large camel-coloured wool coat replaces the fur coat for those who do not have one, or prefer not to have it altered to suit their new shape. The full-cut habit-like coat with hood collar, buttoned high beneath the chin, takes up the fullness in the gathers on the shoulders and hangs like a nun's robes. Two ample pockets with large flaps at bust level complete the effect of this original garment".

125. *Così*, Milano, 13 gennaio 1957. (Venice, Ieri Attualità Archive). "Navy blue is flattering to all figures. This DORMEUIL wool coat with high waist emphasized by a belt starting from one side which ties at the back to form a charming decorative motif is designed by LANVIN-CASTILLO. A line which Princess Grace of Monaco seemed to like: she showed, without showing off lots of exclusive designs, how it is possible to carry out one's duties and devote oneself to one's children with grace and well-mannered dignity".

126. *Così*, Milano, 13 gennaio 1957. (Venice, Ieri Attualità Archive). "A French design with large, round, shawl collar, fastened by four unevenly positioned buttons. The full sewn-in pleats open from the hip to the hem in a motif which makes the walk unusually light and graceful". Design by CLAUDE RIVIÈRE.

126.

few well-known ladies during the last months of their pregnancies.

The clothes which they wore were not particularly elegant, but they were relaxed, hinting at the happy participation of the whole family in the pregnancy.

At the beginning of the Sixties, Paula of Lieges allowed herself to be photographed when clearly pregnant during an official ceremony, dressed in white crepe, while Milly Vitale was pictured at the seaside "with an unusual, very practical swimsuit for the pregnant woman". However, information on this subject was still fairly scarce.

INFORMATION FROM THE SPECIALIZED PRESS

In 1962 *Annabella* (Italian women's magazine trad.) published a small encyclopaedia of beauty, which included a brief paragraph on elegance during pregnancy. "Once, women were forced to wear a kind of dark, unattractive, loose-fitting uniform during pregnancy. Nowadays the whole range of colours, fabrics and styles are available to create an elegant look for the mother-to-be.

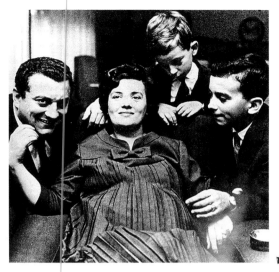

127.

127. *Annabella*, Milan, October 23rd 1960. n. 43 p. 17. (Venice, Ieri Attualità Archive).
The wife of the musician Mario Marini wears a simple but attractive dress with pleats starting from the yoke above the bust.

128. *La Settimana Incom.* Milan 1960, n. 16 p. 11 (Venice, Ieri Attualità Archive.)
Photograph of Paula of Lièges at an official occasion in a white maternity dress.

129. *Annabella*, Milan, August 6th 1961 n. 32 (Venice, Ieri Attualità Archive.)
Milly Vitale walks along the shore in an attractive "romper" style swimsuit with wrap-over front fastened on the left.

128.

129.

130. *Così*, Milan 1957 n. 2. Versions for during and after: the very modern cape seems to be made specially for the expectant mother, and the large darts in the dress can be left loose or drawn in with a martingale as required. The tartan dress cut across the bias can be worn with a belt once the happy event has taken place.

131. *Annabelle*, Zurich, July 1963 n. 32. The feature in which the Swiss magazine presented maternity fashions was entitled "A Stork in view". Various items of advice recommend the use of cotton or linen fabrics in whole colours or tiny patterns or little stripes, which must be washable. Readers are reminded that loose-fitting collars and low necklines are very comfortable in summer.

132. A series of shirt-dresses with square yokes or straight necklines give a feeling of comfortable coolness even for those well on in pregnancy.

133. To distract attention from the "bulge" it's better to draw the eye upward with ribbons, bows, buttons and little neckties.

80

130.

131.

132.

133.

134. *Marie Claire*, Paris, 1961 n. 86 p. 66. (Venice, Ieri Attualità Archive).
The two suits offered by French fashions are particularly elegant and coquettish.

135. *La Donna*, Milan 1963 n. 11 p. 106 (Venice, Library of the CSTC Palazzo Mocenigo).
Dark suit with beige fur trim: the skirt is adjustable and the full jacket is flared with bell-shaped sleeves. The fastening has straps between the buttons which are in fact hidden so that the two strips of fur fit together. (Jeanne D'Albiez).

136. *La Donna*, Milan, 1963 n. 11 p. 108 (Venice, Library of the CSTC Palazzo Mocenigo).
Overshirt with yoke and sleeves all in one piece kimono-style. There are two side-pleats at the front, while at the back there is a fairly full inside pleat. The trousers are adjustable. (Jeanne D'Albiez).

137. *La Donna*, Milan 1963 n. 11 p. 107 (Venice, Palazzo Mocenigo Research Centre Library).
Dark blue dress with wide sleeves caught in by a tight red cuff: the collar and large bow are also red. The dress, with two large pleats at both front and back, opens at the front to show a red panel. (Jeanne D'Albiez).

138. Prè-maman, pleated sundress with stitching on the bodice and skirt with loose pleats. (Venice, 1964, Anna Leandro).

139. *Annabelle*, Lausanne, 1963 n. 32.

135.

136.

137.

A white collar or scarf is advisable at the neck to brighten up the face and make it seem less tired. Bright colours should be avoided unless one has a naturally fresh, pink complexion."

A few years later, a very elegant, exclusive women's magazine, *La donna*, dedicated no less than six pages to "the months of pregnancy", passing them off almost as "a long woman-to-woman chat" to help those "ladies who, during the early months of pregnancy, have lots of little problems of hygiene, clothing and beauty to tackle, with which they do not dare to bother their doctors."

The article dealt with food, make-up, hairstyles, health, exercise and, of course, the wardrobe.

One must be a *coquette* even if one is unable to follow fashions, "especially if, like this year, dresses are tight or fitted at the waist."

Amongst the recommended clothes were skirts with adjustable belts, gathered shirts which should be "cheerful and coquettish" and even "evening outfits" because, the article adds, "you certainly won't be intending to stay shut up in the house for months!"

The feature continues: "Have fun looking for unusual colour combinations. Get your dressmaker to make you something unusual, if you have imagination. Our sketches may suggest some ideas, which you can alter according to your tastes. In

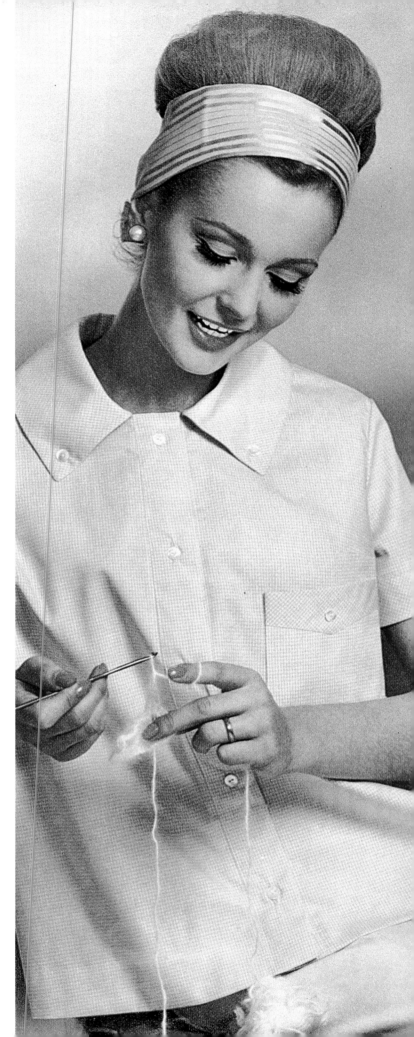

140-143. *Annabelle,* Lausanne, 1963 n. 32.
"Mothers-to-be can, or rather must, be elegant," states a
feature of four colour pages in one of the largest circulation
women's magazines. Maternity fashions spread alongside
the idea that motherhood is beautiful.

85

all cases, until your pregnancy is over, avoid tight clothes. Start off with straight-cut jackets or shirts and then pass on to gathered or pleated overshirts when your girth increases. If you find the pregnant woman's wardrobe boring, make up for it with a bag, an article of jewellery, shoes or gloves. It's important to keep your morale high.

As for coats, cloaks are still in fashion: make the most of this."

THE IDEAL OUTFIT....
OUT OF BOUNDS

For the *brassière*, the suggestion was a good "comfortable but supporting model, without wiring, and with very wide straps," while for the abdomen the ideal is "an elastic girdle, designed especially for the mother-to-be, which supports without being tight."

86

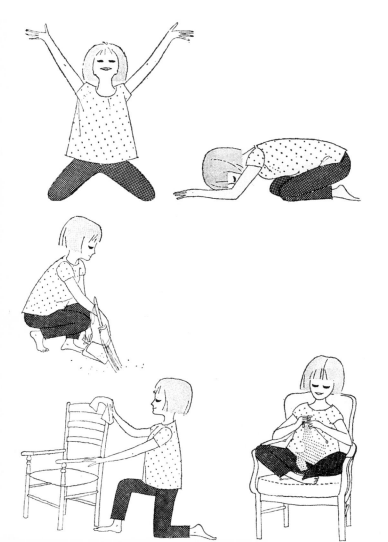

144. *Amica*, Milan, May 15th 1966 n. 20. (Venice, Ieri Attualità Archive.)
Pierre Cardin dress for expectant mothers: desirable, cool, and in a colour which "suits" everybody, turquoise. An informal dress, suitable for wear from Spring onwards, feminine in style and designed especially for this particular occasion. It can always be transformed "afterwards" by drawing it in at the waist with a gros-grain belt in two colours such as yellow and white. It is in woollen cloth with a *roulot* collar, two large slanting pockets and yoke trimmed with a double-stitched slit.

145. M. RISTICH-M. VULLIEZ. *I genitori moderni* (Modern Parents), Florence, Sansoni, 1966, p 53-57. "Aspettarlo".
The pictures show the various activities of a healthy pregnant woman: exercises, housework, and knitting. Recommended wear for the house are "trousers, with a corduroy tunic or loose overshirt to hide the belly and hips."

Finally, the article pointed out that "the ideal garment.... especially during the last months, when the abdomen becomes bulky," would be a pair of trousers.

These were available in stretch models, with adjustable triangles in the side seams "which allow the waistline to be progressively increased," or, even better, with braces.

"Unfortunately," the article added, "we are living in a world where the conventions do not allow women to wear trousers freely. However in the meantime we advise you to wear them in the house, or to go shopping, or for walks."

Another publication of the time, entitled *Genitori moderni* (Modern Parents) confirms the points made above, showing the model mother-to-be doing exercises or the housework, or knitting in trousers and tunic.

For outdoor wear, on the other hand, women are advised to dress as usual until the fourth month, replacing their tight belts with elastic versions and avoiding full skirts "which thicken the figure." From the fifth month onwards maternity clothes

146. *L'enciclopedia della bellezza e della salute*, Turin, Comp. Edit., 1967 p. 393. "La vita sessuale".
The overshirt, decorated with ruches and ribbons, gives the expectant mother a coquettish look.

147. *Annabelle*, Lausanne, 1970, n. 9; 1968, n. 448. Mini-lenght pregnancy dress. Dress with shirt-front featuring tiny buttons. *Annabelle*, Lausanne, 1968 n. 466; 1969, n. 469. Pants and tunic are also a recommended outfit.

specially designed for pregnant women are recommended, but "if you want to continue to have your clothes made by your dressmaker, today's fashions offer you simple, shaped dresses such as trapezium or baggy styles. However, don't choose light-coloured or showy fabrics since these are not flattering, and it's better to go for small-patterned prints."

CONVICTIONS AND TENSIONS

Amica, a young, serious-minded magazine founded its "Mothers' Club", two fairly unconventional pages, in 1966 on Mother's Day, a festival which was the

148.

150.

149.

La Base. (Mail-order catalogue) 1969. (Venice, Ieri Attualità Archive).
The skirts of maternity dresses have become shorter and they have found their way into the mail-order catalogues.

148. Petticoat for the pregnant woman: even the expectant mother's petticoat must be elegant and, above all, practical. This one is in 40 denier Rhodiatoce nylon trimmed with *Valenciennes* lace. The design includes a special adjustable fastening which makes it suitable for wear even after pregnancy.

149. Milady dress: a dress for the expectant mother to wear on the most formal occasions. In terital-wool fabric, it is fully lined and is gathered onto a Korean collar, with back zip fastening and three-quarter sleeves. The very attractive and elegant floral pattern is the latest word.

150. Maternity outfit in wool fabric. The beige skirt can be adjusted by means of a clip at the front and lacing inside. The tartan tunic has long sleeves and fabric-covered buttons. A practical outift which can also be worn afterwards.

151. Betty dress: suitable for the mother-to-be on all occasions, this dress is in pale brown cloth. It is lined to the waist and has a yoke with ribbing and white collar and buttons.

152. Green dress for the expectant mother in woollen cloth. The central front panel is outlined by stitched motif, and the dress has back zip fastening and three-quarter sleeves. A sober, elegant garment.

153. Patterned dress for the mother-to-be's elegant moments. Charming design in soft crease-resistant angora cloth, with elegant pattern in shades of brown on a white background. Simple cut with yoke, ring-collar and back fastening.

154. Pinafore dress for the expectant mother: a very practical item in camel-coloured wool. Round neckline, back zip fastening, lined bodice and covered buttons.

152. **153.**

154.

latest invention of American consumer's culture. This feature was full of useful information on the subject, and appeared in the magazine every week.

The designs offered were often the creations of great stylists. In the meantime the younger generation, who had taken over the Sixties thanks to the post-war baby boom, were forming such a numerous, noisy group that they were able to impose on the fashion world a new lively, colourful style, which no-one was able to resist. And so everyone, even the elderly, dressed up as teenagers, and pregnant women, in mini-skirts and boots, gave an unusual touch of infantile perversion to their condition.

And so our story reaches 1968, with the tanks in Prague, the massacres in Vietnam, and the assassinations of Martin Luther King and Bob Kennedy. Student protest broke out all over the Western world, spreading outside the school to affect the whole of society.

The passive protest of the "flower people" or hippies was born as a reaction against this violent protest movement, leading to the spread of a pastoral-natural style inspired by popular folklore. Maternity wear featured large printed tunics decorated with little mirrors, coloured glass beads and oriental-style embroidery, gipsy-style dresses, and pioneer overalls.

People started talking about the nude-look, unisex and space: it was now 1969 and the first man had stepped onto the moon, while in Italy the nightmare of the socalled "strategy of tension", with terrorism by extremists of both sides, was starting. In spite of everything, pregnancy .... still lasted nine months.

155. Eloise dress: in wool cloth. Pointed collar and ribbing and stitching to emphasize the flare, and elegant little buttons on the bodice. Simplicity and good taste are the keynotes of this dress, which gives an attractive, calm look.

156. From a Seventies mail-order catalogue.
Trousers, tunics and pinafore dresses for spring pregnancies.
(Milan, Bertarelli Print Collection, photograph by Saporetti).

156.

EVEN DOLLS WEAR
MATERNITY CLOTHES

THE END OF PREJUDICE

Specialized fashions for the mother-to-be, after being sickly-sweet and doll-like for twenty years, underwent a transformation. The credit for all these changes must be divided into lots of small victories: the famous actress or singer who proudly showed off her bulge on the most formal of social occasions; the model who wore *haute couture* in spite of her oversize front, and the casual young student mother in jeans and a "western" shirt belonging to the baby's father.

Aware of the importance of the period of pregnancy in human life, and determined to treat it openly, they made prejudices, superstitions and old wives' tales drop away.

The pessimistic proverbs stating that "an open tomb awaits the pregnant woman" or "however good it may be, a pregnancy is nine months of illness", were shown to be unfounded, and being photographed while pregnant led to no ill effects. Finally, people realized that the pregnant woman was beautiful and her belly erotic, even when naked.

157. *Marie-Claire*, Paris, 1972 n. 236 p 41 (Venice, Ieri Attualità Archive).
Childlike, mini-length maternity dress for the teenage mother-to-be.

158. From an advertisement for Terraillon bathroom scales.

158.

This led to the sometimes unjustified spread of images of this type, where unfortunately the pregnant woman was not always treated with the elegance and respect with which, for example, Gustav Klimt had portrayed her at the beginning of the Twentieth Century.

Women were now in control of their own pregnancies and no longer submitted passively to them as had been the case in the past.

DUNGAREES AND TROUSERS

The average age of mothers at the birth of their first child moved to around thirty, and society was forced to face up to an alarming drop in the birth-rate.

160.

159.

159. Prénatal catalogue for Autumn-Winter 1973-4.
For cold weather, a wool tunic with zip fastening, below hip length.

160. *Elle*, Paris, 1977 n. 1652 p. 10
The style presented can be worn "marvellously.... before, during and after pregnancy.

161. *Marie Claire*, Paris, 1972 n. 235 p. 29 and 139 (Venice, Ieri Attualità Archive.)
Practical, elegant and youthful, the ideas arriving from France seem less provincial and ordinary.

161.

95

163.

164.

The process of ideological levelling which had taken place during the Seventies, which led fashions and exhibitionism to be considered as guilty extravagance, led to a levelling in clothing styles so that "all the clothes look alike, like a kind of uniform" (Castagna and D'Agostino.)

The cult of clothing, visual messages and behaviour came back to life with the video-culture of the Eighties.

Everyone was now able to invent and offer his own look, which was conceived as a way of providing a visual expression of the individual's own life, or of constructing an image with which to identify oneself and which was then communicated to other people. This was an age of "narcicism, individualism and hedonism", where paninari (Italian whiz-kids) coexisted with preppies, the "new poor" with the *nouveaux*

162. Prénatal, advertising material Spring-Summer 1973. Motherhood is lived to the full from beginning to end with equal responsibility by both mother and father.

163.165. From the Prénatal catalogue for Spring 1975: jersey pinafore dress, cloth over-dress and flowered tunic with adjustable trousers.

166. *100 Idées*, n. 64, February 1979. Green poplin tunic and full skirt for a romantic look.

167. *Elle* n. 1643 (Venice, Library of the Centro Studi di Palazzo Mocenigo). This type of Indian dress, used as maternity wear from the mid Seventies, is still very modern since it is pretty and practical at the same time.

168. From the Prénatal catalogue for Spring-Summer 1974. Two cool white dresses for summer pregnancies.

169. From the Prénatal catalogue for Spring-Summer 1974. Denim tunics for casual mothers-to-be.

170. August 1978. The authoress in the fourth month of pregnancy wearing a light Empire-line maternity dress with smocking embroidery on the bodice.

171. *Milleidee*, November 1974 (Venice, Ieri Attualità Archive). Original, elegant knitted maternity dress.

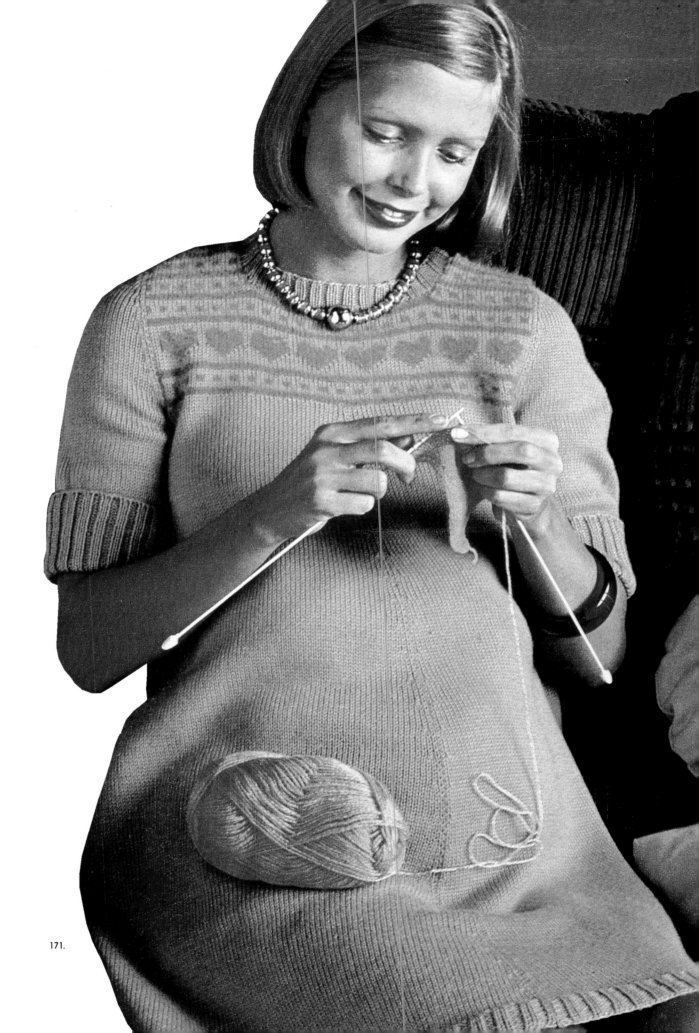

171.

172. *Jardin des Modes*, Paris 1978 n. II p. 75. Short waistcoats, trousers, sleeveless pullovers and smock-type shirts are offered for the young, casual pregnant woman.

173. Prénatal advertising material from the Eighties. The image transmitted is of a strong, vibrant, self-confident woman. Pregnancy is not an illness and so does not stop one joining in sport, apart from working as usual.

174. 1986 ideas by NICOLE CARAMEL for *prêt-à-maman*.

104

175.

176.

177.

Those who are used to wearing trousers certainly have no reason for putting them aside during pregnancy, except perhaps during the last couple of months. There are lots of trousers for pregnant women, cut to keep the line of the legs slender and to keep the size of the belly down. Over them, soft tunics which reach down to cover the hips.

Dresses for pregnant women are always loose-fitting, resting on the shoulders and leaving the body free. The fabrics are always fairly soft, and lengths, even if they follow fashion, are generally proportioned to the special shape which the figure takes on. New experiments can be tried when choosing a dress: fresh colours, for example, may help you to note how your complexion is more luminous. Low necklines may reveal fuller, softer breasts.

During the summer, the seaside and swimming are always advisable for the expectant mother in good health. The swimsuit must allow the greatest possible freedom of movement and exposure to the sun. If you usually wear a two-piece costume, keep on doing so: if you are pregnant there's nothing to hide in the fact that you are expecting a baby. Or go for a simple costume in light fabric with the minimum of support necessary to allow you to move freely.

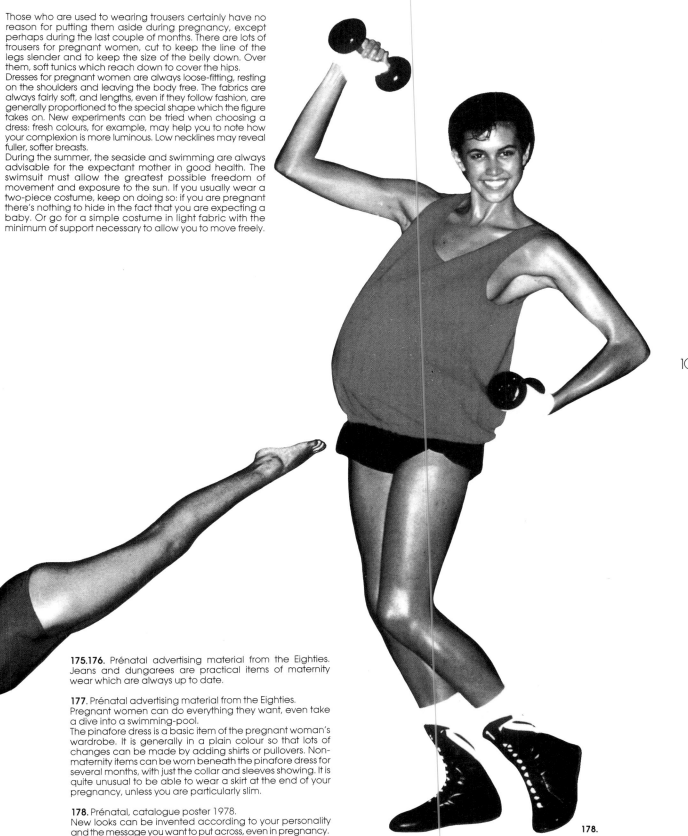

175.176. Prénatal advertising material from the Eighties. Jeans and dungarees are practical items of maternity wear which are always up to date.

177. Prénatal advertising material from the Eighties. Pregnant women can do everything they want, even take a dive into a swimming-pool.
The pinafore dress is a basic item of the pregnant woman's wardrobe. It is generally in a plain colour so that lots of changes can be made by adding shirts or pullovers. Non-maternity items can be worn beneath the pinafore dress for several months, with just the collar and sleeves showing. It is quite unusual to be able to wear a skirt at the end of your pregnancy, unless you are particularly slim.

178. Prénatal, catalogue poster 1978.
New looks can be invented according to your personality and the message you want to put across, even in pregnancy.

178.

106

180.

108

181.

109

179. *100 Idées* n. 8 May 1974. They have respected the divine commandment to go forth and multiply to the letter. The pregnant bride wears a white linen pinafore dress with little pleats worn over a light cotton blouse with full sleeves.

180. The Empire line evening dress worn by Lady Diana, designed by Belville Sasson, is a very elegant garment for the princess's pregnancy.

181. *Moda in Baby*, Modena, 1983, n. 6. Red pullover and trousers for a sporting style pregnancy.

182. *Mamma & Baby* Twice-yearly magazine of fashion, education and psychology. Autumn-Winter 1986, n. 2. This magazine, published by Prénatal, offers a series of different fashion ideas for pregnant women of different personalities, who can identify with and imitate the most famous mothers-to-be of the moment.

182.

183.

riches, and the "aristocrats" with punks, post-rockers or yuppies.

And so normally, pregnant women were clothed in leisure suits and tennis shoes, dungarees with brightly-coloured sashes at the waist, in tangas, shorts or trousers, or in kimonos or *charleston* tunics.

EVEN DOLLS HAVE BABIES

Towards the middle of the 1980s, Karl Lagerfeld, "the most cultured designer, paternally designed high-waisted dresses trimmed with white ermine, suitable for softly regal mothers to be", because his most famous model, Pat Cleveland, "who made all her colleagues change speed at fashion parades, forcing them to move with languid slowness," was three months pregnant (Aspesi).

The gyms, which had sprung up everywhere in large numbers, were attended more by women than by men, and not with the aim of running vainly after perennial youth, but because they wanted to rebuild their bodies, by means of strategic reinforcement of the muscles, as part of a serious program. All this was to obtain equality with the "stronger sex", not only on the intellectual and psychological level, but in physical matters too.

Men's provocative response was to declare that they were prepared to undergo a male pregnancy, even subsidizing serious scientific research with this aim.

At this point, the writer is convinced that the history of maternity clothes is only at its beginning, although a variety of styles, from the aggressive to the sugary, are

183. *Mamma & Baby.* Twice-yearly magazine of fashion, education and psychology. Milan, Autumn-Winter 1986, n. 2

184. *Moda in Baby,* Modena, 1983, n. 6. During the Eighties fashionable dress became a possibility even with the bulge.

185.

already available. They are all decidedly feminine, calculated to make even those who are not pregnant feel like putting on a false belly (as had been the case at the end of the Eighteenth Century).

So, for example, the singer Loredana Bertè was able to turn up at the Sanremo Festival in 1986, accompanied by a group of show-girls, every one of them with a shocking fake belly.

In the same year, a famous toy producer, Mattel, launched a big novelty: a doll in their family became pregnant. All the greatest fashion designers declared themselves willing to create a wardrobe suitable for the first doll in the world to be in the family way.

In the hands of the little girls who, on the verge of the year 2000, play with that body of an adult, pregnant doll, maternity fashions may really develop and come up with surprising ideas.

185. *Mamma & Baby*. Twice-yearly magazine of fashion, education and psychology. Milan, Autumn-Winter 1986, n.2
Bright colours, tartan fabrics, a stand-up collar and a white bib: the conventional but youthful style of Lady Di.

186. Tom Tierney, *Princess Diana and Prince Charles*. London, Dover, 1985, p. 12 (Venice, Ieri Attualità Archive).
This cut-out book with the silhouettes of the two members of the English royal family and a variety of outfits to be interchanged, also included two dresses worn by Princess Diana during pregnancy.

186.

187. 1986, MATTEL launched the "mother-to-be" doll complete with maternity wardrobe onto the toy market for the "Famiglia Cuore" series.

APPENDIX

GLOSSARY

ITALIANO	ENGLISH	FRANÇAIS	DEUTSCH
Balza	**Flounce**	Ruche	Falbell
Basca	**Basque**	Basque	Schoss
Baschina	**Girdle**	Corselet	Leibchen
Berta	**Wide collar, bertha**	Fichu	Berthe, Schulterkragen
Blusante	**Blousing**	Blousant	Blusig
Braghetta o Finta	**Fly**	Braguette	Schlitzübertritt
Busto	**Girdle**	Gaine	Korsett
Cappa	**Cape**	Pelerine	Kappe
Corpino	**Bodice**	Corsage	Mieder
Crinolina	**Crinoline**	Crinoline	Krinolina
Falda	**Tail**	Pan	Schoss
Gonna	**Skirt**	Jupe	Rock
Gonna pantalone	**Pantskirt**	Jupe culotte	Hosenrock
Gravidanza	**Pregnancy**	Grossesse	Schwangerschaft
Grembo	**Lap**	Sein	Mutterleib
Guaina	**Corset**	Guaine	Hüfthalter
Incinta	**Pregnant**	Enceinte	Schwanger
Linea Impero	**Empire line**	Ligne empire	Empirelinie
Paniere	**Hoops**	Panier	Hüftpolster
Pantalone	**Trousers**	Pantalon	Damenhosen
Prematerno	**Maternity dress**	Pré-maman	Umstandskleid
Punto vita	**Waist**	Taille	Taille
Ripresa	**Dart**	Pince	Abnähner
Strascico	**Train**	Traine	Schleppe
Tunica	**Tunic**	Tunique	Tunika
Velluto	**Velvet**	Velour	Samt
Verdugale	**Farthingale**	Vertugadin	Wulst

ESPAÑOL	РУССКИЙ	诠	释	
Lechuguilla	ОБОРКА	边饰	フラップ	
Faldón	ПОЛА		ラッフル 、ひだ	
Faldón	ПОЛА	紧身上衣	ペプラム	
Echarpe	КАШНЕ-КОСЫНКА	宽圆花边领	フィッシュー 、ショール	
Ablusado	АПУСК (С НАПУСКОМ)	衬衫式样	オーバーラップ 、ブラウジング	
Bragueta	ФАЛЬШИВЫЙ КАРМАН ПАНТАЛОНОВ	盖	フライ	
Corsé	КОРСЕТ	紧身胸衣	コルセット	
Esclavina	МАНТИЯ	外套	ケープ	
Corpiño	КОРСАЖ	紧身围腰	ボディス	
Miriñiaque	КРИНОЛИН	衬裙	クリノリン 、クリノリーヌ	
Faldón	СКЛАДКА	下摆	テール	
Falda	ЮБКА	裙子	スカート	
Falda pantalones	ЮБКА-ПАНТАЛОНЫ	裙裤	キュロット スカート	
Embarazo	БЕРЕМЕННОСТЬ	怀孕期	妊娠	
Regazo	ЛОНО / НАКЛАДКА	腰裙	腹部	
Faja	ОБОЛОЧКА	紧身衣	ガードル	
Embarazada	БЕРЕМЕННАЯ	怀孕	妊婦	
Linea imperio	СТИЛЬ-АМПИР	拿破仑时代的式样	エンパイアー ライン	
Panier-Miriñiaque	КАРКАС	裙撑	パニーア	
Pantalones	ПАНТАЛОНЫ	长裤	パンタロン 、ズボン	
Premamá	ПЛАТЬЕ ДЛЯ БЕРЕМЕННОЙ ЖЕНЩИНЫ	孕妇服装	妊婦服, マタニティードレス	
Tailla	ТАЛИЯ	腰围	ウエスト	
Pinza	СКЛАДКА	省位	ダーツ	
Cola	ШЛЕЙФ	拖裙	トレーン	
Túnica	ТУНИКА	束腰外衣	チュニック	
Terciopelo	БАРХАТ	天鹅绒	ベルベット 、ビロード	
Vertugado	ФИЖМЫ	衬架	ベルチュガダン 、ファーチンゲール	

117

BIBLIOGRAPHY

BOOKS

N. Aspesi, "Quel candido collo", *La Repubblica*, 16 marzo 1984.

A. Bony, *Les Années 50*, Paris 1982.

A. Bony, *Les Années 60*, Paris 1984.

G. Butazzi, *1922-1943. Vent'anni di moda italiana*, Milano 1981.

F. Cappi Bentivegna *Abbigliamento e costume nella pittura italiana*, vol. 2, Milano 1981.

C. Cavattoni, *La quistione de' guardinfante destata a Venezia nel luglio del 1773...*, Verona 1774.

L. Castagna e R. D'Agostino, *Look Parade. Gli smodati anni '80*, Milano 1985.

M. Contini, *Cinquemila anni di moda*, Milano 1977.

L. Dalle Nogare e L. Finocchi, *Nascere, sopravvivere e crescere nella Lombardia dell'Ottocento*, Milano 1981.

G. D'Assailly, *Les 15 revolutions de la mode*, Paris 1968.

D. Davanzo Poli, "Non vestivamo prémaman", *Il femminile*, Venezia aprile 1978, n. 4, pp. 54-55.

D. Davanzo Poli, "L'abbigliamento in gravidanza, parto e puerperio", *Nascere a Venezia*, catalogo della mostra, Torino 1985.

Donna Clara, *Dalla cucina al salotto*, Torino-Genova 1926.

Donna Letizia, *Il saper vivere*, Milano 1960.

L. Ercolani, *Igiene della sposa, ossia ragionamenti popolari intorno alla gravidanza, al parto, alla lattazione*, Brescia 1840.

E. Ewing, *History of twentieth century fashion*, London 1986.

E. Ewing, *Dress and undress*, London 1981.

M. Ferro, *La donna dal sesso debole all'unisex*, Milano 1970.

J. Gelis, *L'arbre et le fruit. La naissance dans l'Occident moderne (XVI-XX)*, Paris 1984.

E. e G. Goncourt, *La donna nel Settecento*, pp. 11-12, Milano 1983.

C. Hall, *The thirties in Vogues*, London 1983.

C. Hall, *The forties in Vogues*, London 1985.

Y. Knibiehler e C. Fouquet, *L'histoire des méres du moyen-âge à nos jours*, Paris 1980.

La base, catalogo, Milano 1969.

La famosa storia de' cerchi delle donne tradotta dal francese, Venezia 1725.

R. Laker, *Riflessi di seta*, Milano 1986.

La moda, ossia dell'uso e dell'abuso di busti che adornano il bel sesso..., Parma 1789.

La Rinascente, catalogo, Milano 1925.

R. Levi-Pisetzky, *Storia del costume in Italia*, vol. 4°, Torino 1964-1968.

F. Libron e H. Clouzot, *Le Corset dans l'art et les moeurs du XIII au XX siècles*, Paris 1933.

Olivia, *Annabella Bellezza*, Milano 1962.

V. Piccinni, *Le elegantissime*, Milano 1922.

B. Piergiovanni, *Enciclopedia dell'abbigliamento femminile*, vol. 2°, Milano 1924.

E. Pillon, *La vie de famille au dix-huitiéme siécle*, pp. 29, 30, 32, Paris 1923.

M.A. Racinet, *Le costume historique, France, XVIIIe siècle*, p. 5, Paris 1888.

F. Sapori, *Domenico Baccarini pittore*, Torino 1921.

M. Sichel, *1950 to the Present Day*, London 1979.

Tu Donna, Milano 1967.

A. Witte, *La sarta moderna*, s.d., Milano.

MAGAZINES

1786-88: *La donna galante ed erudita*, Venezia.

1811-44: *Corriere delle dame*, Milano.

1832-48: *La moda*, Venezia.

1840-45: *Il gondoliere*, Venezia.

1840-45: *La moda*, Venezia.

1868: *Il giornale delle donne*, Torino.

1872: *La novità*, Milano.

1876: *Il monitore della moda*, Milano.
1876: *La novità*, Milano.
1876-80: *Il Bazar*, Milano.
1876-80: *L'illustrazione italiana*, Milano.
1884-85: *Margherita*, Milano.
1886: *Il monitore della moda*, Milano.
1888: *L'illustrazione italiana*, Milano.
1888-1909: *La stagione*, Milano.
1891: *L'illustrazione italiana*, Milano.
1891-1911: *Natura ed arte*, Milano.
1893: *La moda genovese*, Genova.
1896-1903: *Margherita*, Milano.
1897: *L'eco della moda*, Milano.
1897: *Moda illustrata*, Milano.
1903: *Corriere delle signore*, n. 11, Milano.
1903-11: *Pro familia*, Bergamo.
1905: *L'eco della moda*, Milano.
1905: *Regina*, n. 3, 11, Napoli.
1907: *Les modes*, Paris.
1909: *Femina*, Paris.
1909-10: *Moda illustrata*, Milano.
1911: *La Stagione*, Milano.
1911-20: *La mode illustrée*, Paris.
1912: *Femina*, Paris.
1912-13: *Regina*, Napoli.
1912-20: *Cultura ed arte*, Milano.
1914: *Femina*, Paris.
1914: *La novità*, Milano.
1914: *La stagione*, Milano.
1914-17: *Il ricamo*, Milano.
1917: *Il giornale delle donne*, Torino.
1920-25: *Femina*, Paris.
1921: *Jardin des modes*, Paris.
1922: *Mademoiselle*, Bruxelles.
1924: *La lettura*, n. 9, Milano.
1925: *Au printemps*, Paris.
1927: *Scena illustrata*, n. 15-20, 23-24, Firenze.
1928: *Femenil*, Buenos Aires.
1928: *Figaro*, Paris.
1928-33: *Femina*, Paris.
1930: *Excelsior*, Milano.
1930-31: *La biancheria elegante*, Milano.
1930-31: *Figaro*, Parigi.
1931: *La lettura*, n. 8, Milano.
1931-34: *Jardin des modes*, Paris.
1933: *La donna, la casa, il bambino*, n. 3, 5, 8, 10, 11.
1934: *La donna, la casa, il bambino*, n. 4, 3, 6, 8, 10.
1934-35: *La famille*, n. 73-75, Paris.
1934-40: *Dea*, Milano.
1935: *La donna, la casa, il bambino*, n. 4, 5, 8, Milano.
1935-39: *Vogue*, Paris.
1936: *La donna, la casa, il bambino*, n. 1, 8, 9, Milano.
1936-39: *Femina*, Paris.
1937: *La donna, la casa, il bambino*, n. 1, 4, Milano.
1938: *Plaisir de France*, Paris.
1939-40: *Jardin des modes*, Paris.

1940-43: *Fili*, Milano.
1944: *Mes blouses*, Milano.
1944-46: *Smart ideas*, Paris.
1945: *Plaire*, n. 5, 7.
1946: *Bellezza*, Milano.
1946: *Mes blouses*, hiver, Paris.
1946-54: *Emporio artistico letterario*, Venezia.
1947: *Figaro*, Paris.
1948: *Plaisir de France*, Paris.
1949: *Elle*, n. 197, Paris.
1949: *Eva*, n. 35, Milano.
1949: *La settimana Incom*, n. 42, Roma.
1950: *Annabella*, n. 24, 26, 50, 52, Milano.
1950: *La settimana Incom*, n. 5, 9, 29, 30, 36, 38, Roma.
1950-54: *Novità*, Milano.
1951: *Annabella*, n. 4, 6, 43, Milano.
1951: *Bellezza*, Milano.
1951: *Donne eleganti*, n. 9, Milano.
1951: *La settimana Incom*, n. 17, 30, 36, 40, 48, Roma.
1951: *Settimo giorno*, n. 18, Milano.
1952: *Annabella*, n. 20, Milano.
1952: *La settimana Incom*, n. 2, 23, 27, 49, Roma.
1953: *La settimana Incom*, n. 9, 15, Roma.
1953-62: *Linea*, Milano.
1954: *La settimana Incom*, n. 9, Roma.
1955: *Epoca*, Milano.
1955: *La settimana Incom*, n. 8, 9, 17, 40, Roma.
1955-58: *Bellezza*, Milano.
1956: *Annabella*, n. 9, 36, 47.
1956: *Epoca*, n. 283, Milano.
1956: *La settimana Incom*, n. 2, 3, 7, 11, 17, Roma.
1956-58: *Eva*, Milano.
1957: *Così*, n. 2, Roma.
1957: *La settimana Incom*, n. 17, 50, Roma.
1958: *La settimana Incom*, n. 42, Roma.
1958-60: *Grazia*, Milano.
1959: *Eva*, n. 4, 14, 21, 45, 53, Milano.
1960: *Annabella*, n. 43, Milano.
1960: *Eva*, n. 4, 6, 43, Milano.
1960: *La settimana Incom*, n. 16, Roma.
1960: *Vogue*, Paris.
1961: *Annabella*, n. 25, 32, Milano.
1963: *Elle*, Paris.
1963-64: *Bellezza*, Milano.
1966: *Amica*, Milano.
1969-74: *Confezione Italiana*, Milano.
1973-85: *Bella*, Milano.
1974-75: *Elle*, Paris.
1974-75: *100 Idées*, Paris.
1975-79: *Il femminile*, Venezia.
1977-78: *Elle*, Paris.
1978: *Jardin des modes*, Paris.
1980-85: *Marie Claire*, Paris.
1985: *Elle*, Paris.
1987: *Moda*, Milano.

Printed in July 1988 by SAGDOS S.p.A. - Brugherio (MI)
Paper: CTS - Cartiera del Timavo e del Sole S.p.A. - Assago (MI)